IN A LEAGUE OF THEIR OWN

Celebrating Cricket's Great Characters

Mayukh Ghosh

IN A LEAGUE OF THEIR OWN
A Collection of Cricketing Anecdotes
by Mayukh Ghosh

ISBN - 978-93-88887-48-9

First Edition - June, 2019

Published by Flying Turtle, an imprint of
Sristisukh Prokashan LLP, Bagnan, Howrah –
711312

International Edition – November 2019

CricketMash, Amstelveen, Netherlands

Cover and Illustration - Sumit Roy

PREFACE

A few weeks ago, renowned cricket historian David Frith gently asked me: 'Are you a well-to-do businessman or a prince by any chance?'

I had informed him about some recent 'acquisitions'. I had to reply that I was neither. Nor do I have a princely monthly income. What's more, my father is no millionaire.

Collecting cricket books and memorabilia while living in India might be tough, but it is still easier than convincing my parents that I must skip school whenever India plays!

That was about 20 years ago. All I had read on the game then was Sunil Gavaskar's Idols and Sunny Days.

However, slowly but surely, in my book, it became the history and the literature of cricket that transformed it into the greatest of all games.

I must thank famous cricket writer Arunabha Sengupta for playing a part in the writing of this book. He was generous enough to send me a few good books, which helped ignite the flame!

These days, I routinely skip watching meaningless ODIs to read on the game. Then one sunny morning (don't ask me why), I just decided to share some of the stories with other cricket enthusiasts I know.

So, by all means, an accidental writer.
Or, perhaps, a narrator.

There are some interesting stories about some interesting cricket personalities. I have enjoyed writing them. I hope you enjoy reading them.

Mayukh Ghosh
January 2019

Giants of the Game

1 RAY LINDWALL

According to *Wisden*, it was 'one of the dreariest batting displays'.

It was orchestrated by one of the finest fast bowlers ever.

Place: England
Year: 1956
Keith Miller, after taking a break on Godfrey Evans' Thames houseboat, took half the team to London for a party and failed to return next morning to play in Australia's match against Hampshire. Miller was supposed to lead the team.

Ray Lindwall found himself temporarily taking Miller's place, but he had only four others to begin the game!

Lindwall was never short of ideas.

This time, he told the quartet: 'Don't worry. I've got a few ideas.'

When Hampshire's captain Desmond Eagar asked about toss, Lindwall said, 'We can't toss, Desmond. The pitch is too wet.'

He knew the pitch was dry but precious minutes were wasted as the umpires inspected.

The toss eventually happened. Lindwall knew he had to win it.

'And that's easy', he said.

Eagar flipped, Lindwall grunted, then stooped over the coin.

'Yep, tails it is. We'll bat.'

He returned to Mackay and Rutherford: 'You guys can forget about runs today. Just don't get out.'

Miller finally arrived half an hour before lunch. Rutherford and Mackay were still there, playing forward-defensives against half-volleys.

Lindwall is widely regarded as one of the finest fast bowlers in the history of cricket. In 1956, Australia and England played in the Ashes series. It is famous for Jim Laker's 19-90 in the Manchester Test.

2 SAEED ANWAR

A few months ago, Patrick Ferriday (who owns *Von Krumm* publishing and who has written some good books on cricket) was asked to write on a great day of cricket played in the subcontinent, for the new Wisden Cricket Monthly magazine.

He decided to write on a Saeed Anwar innings in Kolkata.

He asked me if I was there watching the match. He wanted to understand how Eden Gardens 'worked' in those days and what an Indian thinks about Anwar.

By 1999, I had kind of figured out that this man had scored about half a million runs against India—more than fifty per cent of them being scored in Sharjah.

Saeed Anwar, on good days, was majestic.

He somewhat struggled against the Australians and South Africans but, in ODIs in Asia, no one ever batted like him.

What if his father didn't return from Tehran just before the hostage crisis?

What if he, like one Mohammad Azharuddin, was not sent to stay with his grandparents?

What if he had not taken a last moment decision to not go to the U.S. to study computer engineering?

And what if he failed that Wellington Test in 1994?

Well, India would have won a few more matches.

And a gifted stroke-player would not have defeated typhoid and/or malaria so quickly to recover in the nick of time for the 1996 World Cup.

And, perhaps, Patrick Ferriday would have taken more time to find the 'right subject'

Saeed Anwar was a leading batsman in the 1990s. He was often at his best in Sharjah and against India.

3 TOM WILLS

Just weeks before the English team arrived to play in Australia, the father of the best Australian cricketer quietly took his son away to a remote location so that he could not take part in the matches.

If he had not done so, the history of cricket could have been slightly different.

Tom Wills was educated at Rugby School in England. His father thought that Tom would get the best education there and hence, at the age of 14, Tom set out for a six-month-long journey by sea. He did well at Rugby.

When he returned to Australia in the mid-1850s, he was a changed man. He walked out to the newly opened MCG in his I-Zingari uniform. He batted like no one could. He bowled so fast that batsmen complained that they were not able to see the ball after it left Tom's hand.

He single-handedly developed Australian cricket.

In 1861, his father thought that was enough of cricket for Tom. He had sent him to Rugby so that Tom could become a lawyer. He, along with Tom, left Victoria to settle in central Queensland.

Weeks later, when Tom was in Victoria for some work, 19 white people were attacked and killed by the Aborigines in central Queensland. One of them was Tom's father. The white men took revenge by killing hundreds of Aborigines.

Tom went back to a blood-stained house and slowly developed post-traumatic stress disorder.

Alcohol came to his rescue.

A year or so later, Tom went back to Victoria to play for the team in a match against New South Wales. As the NSW team were on the brink of defeat, their supporters started throwing stones at Victoria's cricketers. One of them hit Tom. He thought that he had seen enough of the 'cricket played by so-called educated white gentlemen'.

He went back to Queensland and formed a team with 10 aborigines, some of whom had killed his father.

On Boxing Day in 1866, he marched his team to the MCG to play against the local club. Tom Willis, the white captain and 10 aborigines.

He wanted to visit England in 1867 but financial difficulties were too big an obstacle to overcome.

The tour did happen in 1868 but by then Tom had been usurped by Charles Lawrence.

Tom played cricket for a few years, but the alcoholism took a toll on him.

In April 1880, he decided to not touch alcohol anymore, but that proved to be fatal. He quickly developed delirium tremens.

On 1 May, he was admitted to a hospital in Melbourne but they couldn't keep him there for more than a few hours.

The very next day, he took his life by stabbing himself with a pair of scissors.

His mother, when asked about her son's death, calmly replied that she never had a son named Tom.

In 2006, Tom Wills was named as one of the '100 most

influential Australians ever'.

Tom's cricket played a part.

But there was more.

On a dark, gloomy evening in 1858, he, accompanied by a few friends, went to a pub in Victoria. There, on a piece of paper, Tom wrote down ten points. Those were later used as rules for 'Australian football'.

Tom invented the game to keep the cricketers fit during winter.

Undoubtedly the first great Australian sportsperson.

The tragic end of Tom Wills can in no way eclipse the fact that he was Australia's first great sportsman.

4 GODFREY EVANS

Perhaps Arthur McIntyre and Keith Andrew were better wicket-keepers, but Godfrey Evans was spectacular.

He may have been matched on the field of play, but off it, he was one of a kind.

One anecdote (fairly sure that not many have heard this one before) pretty much sums up the man:

Late in 1988, Christopher Sandford rung up Evans to seek permission for a biography to mark the latter's 70th birthday.

Evans told Sandford to meet him at the Cricketers Club just off Baker Street in London.

The lunch was good and Evans was happy. He agreed to Sandford's proposal.

The two of them finally emerged back onto the street at about 4 that afternoon, and for one reason or another, Evans—who was about 68 at the time—walked straight into the path of a passing car. There was an ominous thud as he hit the ground, followed by a screech of brakes and then a high-pitched wail from the woman behind the wheel as she leapt out to see an elderly, whiskered figure lying, apparently comatose or even dead, on the street beside her.

Sandford feared the worst. About two seconds later Evans sprang back up like one of those inflatable punching bags that always resume the upright position after being hit, dusted himself off, announced with a broad smile, 'No harm done!', and then invited everyone back inside the club for another drink.

Anyone else would probably have been carted off to a hospital.

Courtesy: Christopher Sandford

Evans was the most famous of all immediate post-war wicketkeepers. He is counted among England's finest.

5 TOM RICHARDSON

In 1963, Wisden identified 'Six Giants of the Wisden Century': W.G. Grace, Victor Trumper, S.F. Barnes, Jack Hobbs, Donald Bradman, and Tom Richardson.

The first five have been the subject of biographies. Some of them have attracted several writers to write on them.

But Tom Richardson didn't have a book on him till 2012.

Eventually, Keith Booth did write one for the 'Association of Cricket Statisticians and Historians', but it is not a full-scale biography.

Tom Richardson was the best of his time, but very little has been written on him.

Moreover, much of the stuff written on him is untrue.

Contrary to popular belief, he was neither of gypsy stock nor born in a caravan. His birth certificate makes that clear. Likewise, his death is unlikely to have been suicide, as most writers writing on him in the 1960s and 1970s have suggested.

The 1911 Census of Population indicates that he was estranged from his wife and lived with his 'housekeeper'. He may have been depressed but there is no concrete proof of his suicide.

Tom played his first cricket at Mitcham, the nursery of Surrey cricket.

There is a story that one end of the wicket was kept dry and the other wet—one for Tom and the other for spinner T.P. Harvey.

But this is probably a figment of someone's imagination.

Herbert Strudwick (another man who learnt his cricket at Mitcham) wrote that there was no truth to this, as did a few other contemporary Surrey cricketers.

Years later, David Frith bought some cricket memorabilia from Tom's son, including a cap that is believed to be the one Tom wore in Test matches.

The Board of Control started (physically) awarding caps in 1899.

It could have been awarded retrospectively, but that seems a bit far-fetched, given how Tom spent his later life.

It probably belonged to someone else.

When we talk about apocryphal cricket stories, Neville Cardus cannot be too far away.

Tom is the subject of at least one such Cardusian 'higher truth'.

But Tom Richardson remains an all-time great—one of the most popular cricketers of the 1890s.

Tom Richardson's record speaks for him. Widely regarded as one of the greatest bowlers in the history of the game.

6 ZED AND SHEP

Great Britain had a pretty ordinary team of athletes for the Montreal Olympics in 1976.

Brendan Foster managed a bronze. That was all.

However, a month before the athletics events started, one fine day in Bristol, people were optimistic.

They had discovered a promising sprinter.

Gloucestershire v Worcestershire in the Gillette Cup.

Norman Gifford won the toss and invited the hosts to put runs on the board.

Sadiq Mohammad and Andy Stovold departed quickly. Then came a 95-run stand between Zaheer Abbas and Mike Procter.

As soon as Procter departed, David Shepherd (who later became a famous umpire) came out to bat.

Like in most winters, in 1975–76, he had successfully put on some weight and the pre-season training had not really helped.

Zed kept calling for singles and Shep obliged. Remorselessly called by Zed, Shep sprinted from one end to the other.

There was the Olympian Great Britain longed for!

His face was red and his shirt was out. Mike Procter near

the boundary couldn't stop himself from shouting 'bloody hell!'.

Suddenly, there was a hush. Shep was in need of attention. He was, in fact, on the point of collapse.
Fielders ran towards him and helped him off the field.
He was stretchered off to the treatment table.
The physiotherapist chuckled and, after a brief examination, said: 'He'll live.'

Zed, meanwhile, did what he loved doing. His century proved to be a match-winning one.

Non-strikers gave up, bowlers gave up, spectators gave up, officials gave up, but Zaheer kept on batting.
Barring Bradman and Hammond (on 'good days'), no one had such desire to score runs.
But his greatest achievement was obviously helping Britain dream on that sunny afternoon in Bristol.

Zaheer Abbas is widely regarded as one of the finest batsmen to have played for Pakistan.

7 BARRY RICHARDS

'It was as if Yehudi Menuhin had called into the Festival Hall on a morning, taken his fiddle on stage, and reeled off faultless, unaccompanied Bach all day, just for the pleasure of the cleaners, box-office clerks, odd electricians, or a carpenter who chanced to be there, without central heating, of course without taking off his coat.'

Tony Lewis on an innings at an empty Lord's in 1974.

'So, who was the greatest batsman you ever played with or against?'
'Richards.', came the reply, without a moment's hesitation.
'Fair enough. I don't think anyone could disagree with that. After all, Wisden named him as one of the five cricketers of the century. King Viv, surely the…'
'Barry. Barry Richards. Not Viv.'

Andrew Murtagh was his teammate at Hampshire.
He later wrote his biography to highlight what the world missed because of the apartheid ban.
It surely was the biggest regret of Barry's life.
Well, not quite.

He found out that nothing could be more distressing than the suicide of a young son.

He also found out that Barry's eyesight began to fail towards the end of his playing career. He was experimenting with contact lenses. When he was hit on the head by Alan Hurst and took time to get to his feet, he was not concussed, as everybody thought—he was scrabbling around to find one of his lenses that had become dislodged!

It was something he had kept quiet about when he was

playing, for obvious reasons.

But he was quick to add: 'Mind you, Barry with two bad eyes was better than the rest of us with two good eyes.'

Barry Richards is often considered as one of the great batsmen. His international career was a short one as it coincided with the apartheid era in South Africa.

8 ALEC BEDSER

What if Alec Bedser had not won that toss?

He was not a captain and there was no match to be played, but it was a very important toss.

He won the toss and remained a medium pacer. His brother Eric lost and became a spinner. There was no place for two medium pacers in the Surrey side.

He did all right.

In 1958, towards the end of his career, he was called to bowl a few special deliveries in Lord's.

Those were way more important than most of his deliveries in top-level cricket.

The custodians of the game (read Gubby Allen and Don Bradman) were so concerned about chucking that they started filming bowlers randomly.

Bedser was called so that they could film his action and use it as a role model.

All that just because he had won that toss!

Alec Bedser is regarded as one of the best medium-fast bowlers in the history of the game.

9 GRAHAM MCKENZIE

At $190 a Test, none of the Australians who beat the West Indies so convincingly in 1968–69 became particularly rich.

One of them, however, was about to take the largely untravelled route of making his game his profession.

During the 1968 Ashes tour, Graham McKenzie signed a three-year contract with Leicestershire.

Alan Connolly followed him with a similar contract with Middlesex.

The counties, for the 1968 season, had endorsed for the Immediate Registration Rule, which surely expedited the recruitments.

What McKenzie (and Connolly) had undertaken was unique.

There had been many successful Australians in county cricket during the immediate post-war years and throughout the 1950s, but they had long left their Australian cricketing days behind.

McKenzie and Connolly were active cricketers and regulars in the Test team.

The two fast bowlers were about to undertake the

routine of cricket throughout the year.

The risks were there but they had no choice but to play overseas if they wished to earn more than subsistence income.

They made their county debuts in 1969 and did well.

McKenzie earned £3000. Connolly got £1750. Way higher than what they got in Australia.

When they started their second season in 1970, they had been playing the game continuously since October 1967. After starting well, Connolly broke down.

It was bad news for both of them as the 'opposition' found something to talk about.

They somehow laboured on till the 1970-71 Ashes.

Trying to earn a living in a semi-amateur cricket economy, they had bowled themselves into the ground.

Graham McKenzie showed the path for many of the Australian cricketers—most notably, Ian Chappell.

When the SACA, after the conclusion of the first Test of the 1969–70 series, wanted to add a fifth Test, it was McKenzie and Chappell who opposed.

For once, they had the guts to refuse their cricket board.

Graham McKenzie ended up with 246 Test wickets, just two behind Richie Benaud's then record tally (for Australia) of 248.

There were many who echoed David Frith's thought on this:

'I reckon the Board dropped him just as he was about to overtake Benaud's wicket-taking tally, so besotted with Benaud were they.'

In Western Australia, they call him 'the man without a single enemy'.

'Garth' McKenzie was the leading Australian fast bowler in the 1960s.

10 LEN HUTTON

Bradman scored 234. Barnes scored 234.
Edrich scored a century.
England lost by an innings and 33 runs.

However, the talking point was a 37 scored off 39 balls in 24 minutes.
He took Freer and Miller to the cleaners.
The spectacle lasted till the last ball before lunch when he accidentally hit his own wicket.
In *The Guardian*, Neville Cardus wrote: 'This was a crying shame, challenging justice and philosophy.'
The innings, according to him, 'elevated a match of mass production and utility to the realms of fine art.'

A young Harold Pinter heard about it on the radio. The voice of Alan McGilvray. The usual story of England struggling and Norman Yardley fighting it out all alone. The innings had a lasting impact on him. In three run-on lines entitled 'Poem', Pinter enshrined the first professional captain of England in a world that had vanished forever: 'I saw Len Hutton in his prime | Another time | Another time.'

Years later, he confessed, 'Sometimes, when I feel a little exhausted with it all and the world's sitting heavily on my head, I pick up a *Wisden* and read about Len Hutton's 37 in 24 minutes at Sydney in 1946.'

Apart from that 37, Len Hutton scored another 40,103 runs in top level cricket, with the aid of a small matter of 129 centuries.

P.S. He was possibly the first man to suggest four-day Test matches, way back in 1939. At the end of the timeless Test in Durban in 1939, he said to Hammond: 'Four days is plenty for a Test match, skipper. Convinced of it.'

Len Hutton is widely regarded as one of the greatest opening batsmen ever.

11 WALLY HAMMOND

It was Geoff Edrich's debut in first-class cricket.

He had been given lbw in the previous match he played that season when he had hit the ball.

In this match, when on 20, he played a forward defensive to a ball from Tom Goddard and got a faint tickle onto the pad and up to short leg.

The bowler shouted. Everyone else standing around the bat shouted as well.

The umpire gave it not out.

Wally Hammond was standing at slip when all this happened. At the end of the over he walked down the pitch, swinging his arms like a prince. He didn't look at Edrich. He just walked on and Edrich could hear his voice: 'Your brother Bill (by then a Test cricketer) wouldn't have done that.'

Geoff went to the other end, waved his bat at one straight ball, and the castle went down.

He just wanted to get out. He wanted a tunnel. From that day forward, he never stayed when he got a touch.

That's how you sledge on the field of play.

Wally Hammond is often regarded as the best ever English batsman.

12 ALAN DAVIDSON

'Just one more over, Al'

'I can't, Richie. I'm done.'

'But just try another one, Al. That was a beautiful ball that last over you sent down to Bailey. Come on Al, here's the ball.'

'Where's the ball, Richie? I can't see it.'

Then he would snatch it from Benaud and bowl that over.

Alan Davidson was a great all-rounder. His record speaks for him.

But what he did in Johannesburg in 1957 is important yet little-known.

After three days of cricket, Ian Craig's Australia were 7-307 in reply to South Africa's 470-9 declared.

The players wanted to relax but the manager Jack Norton had imposed a 10 pm curfew. South Africans were also under curfew, but for them it was 11:30 pm.

But that evening, Davidson thought he had had enough of Norton's rules. He told Les Favell, 'Look, if I don't get out, I'm going to go off my rocker. Let's go out tonight. Bugger the curfew.'

They got a car from Ken Funston and drove 35 miles towards Pretoria for a look-see. Their innocent excursion ended at 1 am.

When they checked with the concierge for their room-key, all they got was a note: 'Report to me. I've got your keys. Norton.'

They had a rather unprintable discussion. Once it ended, the duo headed for the home of the Rosenbergs, who were local cricket lovers and had entertained the team at dinner the previous night.

They got a bed there.

The next morning, as soon as they reached the ground, one of their teammates said: 'You two are in trouble. You're on the first plane home.'

Davidson got more determined and bowled like a man who suddenly wished to be considered indispensable. He took three wickets before lunch and then had another meeting with Norton.

He knocked the door, this time with more confidence: 'I believe you want to see me Jack?'

'Where were you last night?'

'I was at the Rosenbergs.'

'Hmm, that's Favell's story too.'

Davidson went to the window and found Mr Rosenberg. 'Why don't you ask him?'

'Well, he says so too. So, I suppose I've got to accept it.'

Davidson took 6-34, thus saving the match and providing empirical evidence that late nights need not impair performance.

The curfew was repealed.

It was Davidson who inspired the likes of Sobers, Botham, and Warne.

Alan Davidson, along with Wasim Akram, is often considered as the best ever left-arm fast bowler.

13 RAY ILLINGWORTH

'I've got something for you to do for me. You are the players' representative. I want to know if the players want Boycs as captain.'

Ray Illingworth to Geoff Cope.

Headingley, 1979.

And thus started the most pathetic and long-lasting turmoil in post-war English cricket.

'I don't think that's fair, Raymond.'

'Well, don't you worry about it. You're the representative, you're doing something for me. I'll deal with it from then on. But I want to know where I stand.'

13 for a change, 4 for an abstain.

'I'm still not happy, Raymond. But this is what you asked me for.'

'Thanks. I'll deal with the rest.'

'Because I was still not officially the cricket manager of Yorkshire, I asked the senior capped player, Geoff Cope, to check with his colleagues…', is what he wrote in his autobiography *Yorkshire and Back*.

It was published in June 1980.

In 1987, he released *The Tempestuous Years*.

In that, he wrote: 'Boycott's captaincy was causing a fair amount of unrest at Yorkshire, particularly among the players. I knew it was a problem that would have to be sorted out one day—one way or another.

'But then I heard that off-spinner Geoff Cope had conducted a round robin amongst the Yorkshire players to ask whether they wanted Geoffrey as captain. It has been suggested in some places that in some way I instigated this poll. Well, that is totally untrue. I didn't even hear of it until it had already taken place.'

Boycott was predictable. In fact, one could always expect him to be rather cold.

Illingworth was perhaps more complex. He was shrewd and stubborn.

And as captain of England, even more stubborn than Douglas Jardine.

Ray Illingworth was a successful captain of the England team. He was also a giant in English domestic cricket.

14 DENIS COMPTON

8 July 1948.

Old Trafford.

The Lindwall bouncer is on target. The batsman misses the hook. He leaves the field bleeding to get his eyebrow stitched and plastered.

He goes back out and is greeted by another bouncer. But he handles this one in a better way.

At the end, he has 145 not out to his name.

Later that year, in South Africa, he hands over a suitcase full of letters to journalist Reg Hayter. Of course, he is too busy to even open the suitcase.

Hayter immerses himself in those letters and finds many lucrative offers for the cricketer.

News of the World offered him £2,000 for an article. Two months later, not getting a reply, they have withdrawn the offer.

Hayter sends the important letters to his publisher friend in England. He convinces the cricketer to sign a £1,000 per year deal with Brylcreem. It paves the way for many to secure contracts.

In 1961, Johnny Haynes of Fulham became the first to secure a deal of £1,000 per week.

2 February 1955.

Adelaide.

Godfrey Evans hits the winning runs to win The Ashes for England.

'What have you done?', shouts the non-striker.

Evans looks perplexed.

It turns out to be that an American investor had offered the non-striker a fabulous sum of £100 if he could make the winning hit. The only condition was that no one else should know this.

'Never saw a more bitter man at a team piss-up than him that night.'

Denis Compton was a hero, on and off the field. He kept things simple and enjoyed playing the game.

When Nick tried very hard to impress his grandfather with nice orthodox stroke-play but failed to do so, an exasperated Denis shouted: 'For God's sake, hit the bloody thing!'

Denis Compton was a popular English batsman who is forever remembered for his exploits in the 'Brylcreem Summer' of 1947.

15 HEDLEY VERITY

Verily, virile, Verity.
With wonderful skill and dexterity
In a very few overs
He made Notts the rovers
A record to hand to posterity.

J.B. Fecknall published this in the *Nottingham Evening News*, four days after Hedley Verity took 10 for 10 in a first-class match.

When the season of 1928 commenced, Hedley Verity was a medium pace bowler for Middleton in the Lancashire League.

It was George Hirst who suggested him to play in the Lancashire League and change his style of bowling.

There were too many medium pacers in Yorkshire. So, Verity changed his style and became a spinner.

Wilfred Rhodes was nearing the end of his career. Hirst wanted a good replacement.

Verity's first championship appearance was closely watched by Rhodes.

At the end of the match, Rhodes said two words to the Yorkshire committee: 'He'll do.'

And there was no looking back.

There weren't many who had such a singular intent in life. Playing for Yorkshire was what Verity lived for.

There hung a plaque above his bed in his room:

'They told him it couldn't be done, he made up his mind that it could—and he did it.'

A rather concerned father wrote, 'His time was so fully occupied in the cricket field that he had no time for anything else. Any friends he found were expected to, if they wished to retain his friendship, go with him to the cricket field. Some joined the club, but I am afraid most of them found companionship elsewhere. For the same reason, he had no girlfriends. He could not afford to waste his time on such business.'

He hired a private tutor for his son.

'It's no use, dad, you're wasting your money. I've made up my mind to someday play for Yorkshire.'

The greatest left-arm spinner.

Hedley Verity is widely considered as the greatest left-arm spin bowler. He was tragically killed in action during World War II.

16 JACK FINGLETON

1942.
Wartime.

Australian Army's Public Relation Unit in Townsville.

The 33-year-old was struggling. He somehow managed to avoid charges of being AWOL when he went missing during the Japanese midget submarine attack on Sydney harbour.

He was supposed to have been on duty but instead he was visiting his new wife Philippa.

He was caught and transferred north, well away from his family. And there, he started to write on the game he loved.

'There are two teams out there. One is trying to play cricket and the other is not.'

In his book *Cricket Between Two Wars*, Pelham Warner indirectly accused Jack Fingleton of leaking this to the fellow pressmen.

Fingleton wrote to Warner to be absolutely sure.

Warner confirmed that it was indeed Fingleton who broke the news to the press.

Fingleton denied but Warner wanted concrete proof.

Fingleton didn't want to give that to him. Instead, he wanted to write his own version of the story.

He was a decent journalist, who had never written any book. He needed advice. Neville Cardus encouraged him and 'Fingo' started to write.

Once the initial manuscript was ready, he had it sent to 'Pedlar' Palmer, his sports editor at *The Sydney Guardian*, to have a look.

The manuscript never arrived at Palmer's office and Fingleton, rather stupidly, didn't have another copy.

Alone in north Queensland, away from his family, and with all his efforts to write a book going in vain, he went into depression.

But his urge to become a cricket writer proved to be too powerful against the depression and he wrote the book all over again.

At the same time, Ray Robinson was writing a book and he was covering a bit of Bodyline in that. Plus, he already had a publisher.

Fingleton didn't have a publisher and wasn't sure he could compete with someone like Robinson.

Fingleton persuaded Cassell to publish the book. It was published in late 1946, just three months after Robinson's *Between Wickets*.

Both books did well and after all these years, Fingleton's *Cricket Crisis* usually makes the 'Top 10' lists everywhere, often by people who haven't read it.

He didn't name the culprit who leaked the Bodyline story, however. He waited till 1978 and then, in his book on Victor Trumper, he revealed the name of the culprit.

He got the information from the journalist who wrote the original story back in 1932–33.

Complex, stubborn, short-tempered, but often brilliant as a cricketer and analyst.

Jack Fingleton was a very good cricketer and, in latter life, a well-respected journalist/writer. He was somewhat obsessed with Bradman.

17 JASON GILLESPIE

Trent Bridge, 2005

'It was the chairman of selectors Trevor Hohns who delivered the news. We chatted for a while, and Ricky came over and asked: "Has Trevor spoken to you yet?"

'I indicated that he had. Ricky just said "okay" and walked off. There was no "Bad luck, mate" or pat on the shoulder, which confirmed for me that I no longer had the support of my captain. All through the tour, I'd this niggling feeling that I'd fallen from favour, and at that moment was 100 per cent sure that Ricky didn't want me in the side. Why he didn't have some sort of chat with me, I don't know. It's bewildering…'

Adelaide, 1992–93

A 17-year-old was the mainstay of the batting line up of the Grade D and Grade E team of Adelaide Cricket Club. He always used to tell his teammates that he would make his debut for South Australia before turning 20 and would play for Australia before turning 22. Everyone had a good laugh whenever he mentioned this.

Then, one night, he had enough of all this. He marked a long run-up and then started to bowl as fast as he could.

The coach was stunned and decided to give him a go with the A team.

But the cricketer's dad (a selector of the lower grade teams) thought it was a mistake—he felt his son was not ready for such serious cricket.

When his son made his debut for the A team, he watched him bowl throughout the first day and at the end of it, nodded and said: 'He's proven me wrong. I know nothing about cricket.'

His son indeed made his debut for SA before turning 20 and for Australia before he turned 22.

He could bowl. He could, in fact, bowl really well. At his best, he was the best.

'Dizzy' Gillespie, when on song, was fast and accurate. There were not many better than him when he was at his peak.

18 DICKIE BIRD

He suddenly threw his arm out, causing the bowler to put on the brakes. Then he toddled down the pitch and removed a microscopic piece of turf or something.

No, not the batsman. The umpire.

Later, he ran backwards at a very quick pace when a ball was hit some distance from him and collided with a fieldsman behind him.

Poor Kallicharan was about to bend down to field the ball at mid-on…

He found it difficult to adjust to Dennis Lillee's shortened run-up midway through an over.

Thereafter, for every ball Lillee bowled, even off his long run-up, this umpire kept sneaking untrusting looks over his shoulder.

H.D. Bird was bloody serious about whatever he did on the cricket field.

In 1983, to celebrate Dickie's 50th birthday, David Frith wrote a charming little piece for The Twelfth Man (Wombwell Cricket Lovers' Society's magazine).

There he said: 'H.D. Bird views the task of deciding whether play should proceed in drizzle or dubious light with the same gravity that Chamberlain applied to the German threat.'

He has written many books on the game and on his own life. He wasn't that serious when it came to writing. The good stories are there but not many of them are true.

Dickie never worried about that. His autobiography sold over a million copies.

Umpire Bird always had a smile on his face, even when, in the 70s and 80s, he was surrounded by fiery fast bowlers and terrified batsmen.

No wonder the cricketing world loves him.

Dickie Bird is the most popular among the men in white coats.

19 MALCOLM MARSHALL

The Essex spin-twins, David Acfield and Ray East, used to wait by his car and offered to carry his bags to the dressing room.

The first time it happened, the bemused bowler asked, 'Why?'

'Well, Mr Marshall, we thought you might consider a couple of half-volleys, and if they're nice and straight, we promise to miss them!'

But there were a few who relished the challenge. One such was former Sussex skipper John Barclay.

Sussex v Hampshire at Eastbourne in 1983.

Sussex 6 for 83 on day one when Barclay joined Imran at the crease.

'Back and across I went. Marshall's arm came over high and fast. Simultaneously, I heard a thud as the ball hit the pitch just short of a length. I sensed it was rearing up towards my chest. Uncertainly I fended at it. The ball passed by my side without causing harm but, as it did so, just brushed my glove on its way through to Hampshire's wicket-keeper, Bobby Parks.'

There was a huge appeal but umpire Shepherd said 'not out' and Barclay didn't walk.

At the end of the over, Barclay met Imran at the other end.

'A brave thing to do, Johnny', he said, 'I think I had better get down that end next over.'

Nick Pocock, the Hampshire captain, strolled past Barclay. 'Did you hit that one?' he asked.

'I'm afraid to say I did', Barclay replied with shame in his voice.

'I thought so', he said and left it at that.

Not quite. He informed the fast bowler about this conversation he had with Barclay.

Luckily for Barclay, Imran was at the striker's end when Marshall started his next over.

As he prepared to deliver the first ball, he stopped suddenly, whipped off the bails, and shouted 'Howzat'.

Barclay was lost in his thoughts and had wandered out of his crease.

This time, even before Shepherd could raise his finger, he started to walk.

But Pocock came running towards Barclay and said, 'No, no, no, we don't play cricket like that in Hampshire. If it's all right, Shep, I'd like to withdraw the appeal.'

And so he did.

At the end of the over, Marshall threw the ball down in disgust and said that he won't bowl anymore.

He came back later that day and at the end of his first over of the new spell, he had one more wicket to his name:

JRT Barclay c Greenidge b Marshall 41

Malcolm Marshall if often considered among the finest fast bowlers the game has ever seen.

20 WALLY GROUT

Steve Waugh started sledging.
Steve Smith started ball tampering.

....

Both 19th century phenomena.
However, one of the finest sledgers in the history of the game—Wally Grout— happens to be a favourite of mine.

Umpire Col Egar once found himself with Grout(y) in a car.
They stopped at some traffic light and Grout said to Egar: 'You get out here, don't you?'
Egar looked out of the window and said: 'No, this isn't my hotel.'
Grout then read him a traffic sign attached to a post: 'Blind pedestrians cross here.'

He didn't spare the crowds either.
In Old Trafford in 1964, a Lancashire member yelled, 'Declare, Simpson, you bastard.'
Grout responded rather drily: 'What about The Oval 1938?'

He was a great sportsman as well.
He didn't run Fred Titmus out in the Trent Bridge Test in 1964 when the latter was on the ground after a collision with bowler Neil Hawke.
The same batsman was again at the receiving end of Grout's magnanimity during the 1966 Melbourne Test.

In an era of rather boring cricket by the likes of Boycott, Mackay, Burke etc., Grout was one of the few who literally kept the game alive.

Little known fact: Much to the delight of many, he even gave a tough time to the eccentric Rowland Bowen. Bowen took years to find out whether he was ATW Grout or AWT Grout…

Wally Grout was a fine wicketkeeper and an amusing character.

21 NASSER HUSSAIN

'I'm sorry Mrs Hussain, it's another boy.'

The Hussains had two boys and had just lost their young daughter. They had hoped for a girl.

But they were happy that the child survived.

A month or so after Shireen Hussain fell pregnant, the doctors in Madras told her there was no hope of the baby surviving.

She was even told, quite brutally, that the baby would have to be flushed down the toilet.

They insisted that there was no hope remaining and she must accept it.

But she didn't. She fought to give the baby a chance to live.

Nasser was born.

Shireen always believed that Nasser became a fighter because of all this.

They moved to England in 1975 but before that, young Nasser had the chance to face Lance Gibbs' bowling in Madras.

Nasser became a sensation due to his skills as a leg-spinner. He even led the England schools' team.

But then, one fine morning, he discovered that he had lost it.

He tried, got frustrated, got depressed, but couldn't salvage the situation.

He decided to become a specialist batsman.

But he would never have become a cricketer were it not for his father and the sacrifices he made. Nasser, till the last day of his career, played to satisfy his father.

He did pretty well, didn't he?

Nasser Hussain led the England team on numerous occasions. He is now a popular television commentator.

22 MIKE ATHERTON

In June 1978, 10-year-old Mike Atherton was summoned by his father.

It was urgent.

A curly-haired David Gower was making his debut.

'See how still he keeps his head.'

Mike Atherton never forgot that.

At the age of eight, he was reading Wilbur Smith. Many years later, when Graeme Hick came to learn this, he said: 'That's why he went to Cambridge and I didn't.'

He was a promising leg-spinner in the Cambridge University team.

He did well enough to get a chance to play for Lancashire.

That dressing-room was full of players who came from the league. They were a bit overawed by Mike's background.

He earned the nickname 'FEC'.

Many thought it meant 'Future England Captain'.

But no, it meant something else: F***ing educated c**t.

He did well. He often inspired the likes of Ambrose, Donald, and McGrath to bowl at their best.

In 2015, Gideon Haigh was requested to write an article for *The Nightwatchman*.

The subject he chose was about writing cricket columns.

He found no one better than Atherton to follow and went to stay with him in his house.

They sat at the same table.

Atherton wrote and filed a cricket column for The Times. Haigh, who watched Atherton's working very closely, also finished writing his piece for The Nightwatchman.

It's not easy to lead a Test team in international cricket.

It's perhaps equally tough to follow in the footsteps of John Woodcock and Alan Lee.

But he has excelled once again.

Mike Atherton led the rather ordinary England team in the 1990s. Later he became a respected commentator and writer.

23 JACKIE MCGLEW

'The South Wales express sped through the Severn Tunnel and on into Glamorgan. I sat, chin cupped in palm, and brooded... and listened. The wheels clattered on:

'"You'll never get a run. You'll never get a run. You'll never get a run." I heard them.

'And I suppose I hated them.

'Yet I hardly dared to contradict them. Cricket had brought me this far, and now I felt that I had failed it; or more correctly, that I had failed all those who had shown confidence in me.

'I had failed them not only at the first time of asking, but at the second—and then at the third.'

Not many cricket books with a better beginning. In fact, the whole book is beautifully written.

But not many know of his skills as a writer. Just as not many know how good a batsman he was.

But Jackie McGlew was special. He was so special that despite having a two-for as his best bowling in FC cricket, he once took a hat-trick in first-class cricket!

Jackie McGlew was a leading South African batsman in the 1950s.

24 FRED TRUEMAN

The young bowler searched for raw pace at the expense of accuracy, as the Yorkshire tradition demanded. As a result, he was in and out of the team for many years.

While describing his debut, Wisden, however, made the error of the century. They wrote 'Trueman, the spin bowler...'

A couple of years later, he cried in the Lord's dressing-room after having an ordinary match against Middlesex.

'I don't think I'll ever make it.'

Six years later, he was in India. While travelling from Calcutta to Bombay, the team shared a flight with Prime Minister Jawaharlal Nehru. The manager sat next to Nehru. He got up only once during the journey. When he came back, he saw Fred sitting beside Nehru and giving him a real ear-bashing about the state of the country!

For the next seven years, he was the best fast bowler in the world.

His hagiographer John Arlott wrote: 'The God of cricket achieved one of his greatest triumphs of creation in Fred Trueman. Stories will be told about him as long as men talk about cricket. No one who ever saw him bowl will be able to forget.'

P.S. Most of those after-dinner tales are apocryphal, but they are bloody good...

'Fiery' Fred was the first bowler to take 300 Test wickets.

25 MONTY NOBLE

'This is not a text-book on cricket. Text-books are all very well in their way but, so far as cricket is concerned, I have not much faith in them. You cannot teach the game by rule of thumb. You may lay down general principles in such works, but in order to be really useful, a separate guide would have to be written for every individual cricketer, because each is virtually a law unto himself. Ability to play the game is a natural attribute. It cannot be taught. If you possess the talent and temperament, you will develop as a matter of course, provided you meet strong enough opposition to draw you out. If you have no inherent cricket in your make-up, no book ever written will help you very far.'

Australia's greatest all-round cricketer (arguably, of course) wrote this 75 years before Sehwag made his Test debut.

In 2013, when Russell Crowe needed a pre-World War I bat for his film *The Water Diviner* (the story of an Australian father travelling to Turkey post-WW I to look for his lost or dead sons), he wanted to have one modelled on what Monty Noble used roughly 10 years before the Gallipoli debacle. He went through all *Wisdens* from the first decade of the 20th century to find the bat Noble used.

All he wanted was to pay a tribute to the best pre-war Australian cricketer.

Monty Noble was a leading pre- World War I cricketer.

26 ARTHUR MORRIS

Whenever there was a discussion about Bradman's famous duck, he used to say: 'Yes, I was there.'
'Were you playing?'
'Yes. I got 196.'

Arthur Morris never regretted anything about his cricket career.

As Australia toured the West Indies in 1955, his wife Valerie, a former dancer, fell seriously ill. Morris was not informed about it—he came to know only after he returned home. Valerie explained that she hadn't wanted to worry him with the suspicion of her breast cancer and waited until his return to seek treatment.

Despite having a breast removed in 1955, the cancer took hold and Morris had to quit the game after averaging 45 in his last series.

'I had to retire. I knew we wouldn't have long together, five years at the outside. The one thing I wanted was to take her to England one last time, which wasn't easy because we had no money, but I was a very lucky man.'

One of his wife's former impresarios sent a cheque for £500. Lindsay Hassett sent another £500 with a note: 'Just pay me back when you can.'

Morris repaid the money and took his wife to England one last time by accepting an offer to cover the 1956 Ashes series for the *Daily Express*.
Valerie died a year later.

An unsung hero whose name should more often be part

of all those discussions about the best left-handed opening batsmen in the history of the game.

Arthur Morris is often regarded as one of the finest opening batsmen in the history of the game.

27 AUBREY FAULKNER

At around seven o'clock on the morning of 10 September 1930, the managing director of the world's first permanent indoor cricket school placed his mouth over the jet of a gas radiator.

The suicide note to his secretary read: 'Dear Mackenzie, I am off to another sphere via the small bat-drying room. Better call in a policeman to do the investigating.'

In 1953, Ian Peebles wrote in his book Talking of Cricket: 'Returning to London, I called on his widow, who told me something which moved me deeply. In the latter days, when he seemed to tire of everything, he had but one unfailing interest. It was to look at the morning paper to see how many wickets, I, his discovery and protege, had taken the previous day.'

He had been active in two nasty wars. He became a pessimist. Slowly, that led to acute depression.

Once upon a time, he could do wonders on the cricket field. He was the greatest all-rounder before the Great War. He remains the only man to score over 500 runs and take 25 or more wickets in a Test series.

A genius. So much so that he managed to play a whole Test match with his trousers held up by a piece of string!

When we discuss about great all-rounders the name of Aubrey Faulkner if often overlooked. Wrongly, though.

28 GEOFFREY BOYCOTT

In 1971, Geoff Boycott scored 2503 runs at 100.12, thus becoming the first English batsman to average 100 in a summer.

His final innings that summer was against Northamptonshire at Harrogate.

Northants had been bowled out for 61 on a pitch, which usually took turn later in the match.

Yorkshire found themselves on 266 for 2 with Boycott batting there on 124.

The bowlers were relaxing, sure that they would comfortably bat the opposition out of the match.

And suddenly they found the two batsmen walking back.

There were murmurs: 'Hang on, is it lunch already? What's going on?'

Boycott walked in and said: 'I've declared.'

'You what?', out came Tony Nicholson from the toilet.

'What do you mean, you've declared? You know what Harrogate's like on the last day?'

Boycott quietly said: 'I've spoken with Ted (Lester, the scorer) and, when I reached 121, I was averaging 100 for the season.'

Nicholson was furious.

He ran back to the toilet, threw something down, pulled the flush and said, 'I've just washed you down there. You big shit.'

Boycott played five or more FC innings against 32 opponents and he failed to score a century against only one of them: Oxford University.

In 1974, he was bowled for 89 by Imran Khan.

Four years later, he was determined to make it count.

He was dismissed for nought in the first innings and he

had to spend the rest of the day watching the other opener and the number 3 batsman getting centuries.

Despite a lead of 343, he decided to bat again. This time he managed only 3 runs.

Instead of declaring, he made all the Yorkshire bowlers bowl at him in the nets all the next morning.

They finished with such a horrendous lead that it was embarrassing.

They could not win the game.

True Yorkshire grit and bloody-mindedness.

Sir Geoffrey Boycott has been one of a kind. A Yorkshire and England legend.

29 VICTOR TRUMPER

'I am concerned with Trumper as an artist, not as a scorer of match-winning runs. You will no more get an idea of the quality of Trumper's batsmanship by adding up his runs than you will get an idea of the quality of Shelley's poetry by adding up the number of lines written by Shelley.' This was what Neville Cardus had to say about Victor Trumper.

His team mate Charlie Macartney had put it perfectly, 'I have one great satisfaction regarding Victor Trumper—I never saw him get old as a cricketer, I say, without hesitation, that he was the best batsman I ever saw. He excelled on any wicket and against any bowling, but beyond his cricket he was a man, a fighter on the cricket field, and a thorough gentleman at all times.'

He lived for only 37 years and ended up becoming 'The Immortal Victor Trumper'.

The George Bedlam photograph of him stepping out to hit the ball is the most famous cricket photo ever.

Victor Trumper has been an enigma. The one cricketer who made all romantics fall for him.

30 WES HALL

On an unpleasantly damp and cold June morning, Wes Hall had slept in and missed breakfast.

His captain Frank Worrell gave him two hard-boiled eggs and a packet of salt on the bus ride to Lord's for the last day of the second Test in the 1963 series.

He bowled a 24-over spell from the pavilion end, lasting from the delayed start at 2:20 pm to the dramatic final over.

In 2013, Tony Cozïer chose this as the finest moment in the history of the Wisden Trophy.

During his schooldays, Cozier opened the batting for Lodge School in Barbados. Hall used to represent Spartan in Barbadian School cricket.

When Cozier first faced Hall, he hit his first ball for four.

Almost 40 years later, Cozier reminded Hall of this incident. Hall smiled and replied: 'You lucky you still living.'

A fast and furious West Indian fast bowler. One of the best among them.

31 NEIL HARVEY

25 November 1958.

Neil Harvey was in his office when the telephone rang.

It was Richie Benaud.

'Guess who's captain?', asked Benaud.

'You are', Harvey replied.

'That's right. I am sorry. I thought you should have got it.'

Richie and I had been mates for years, so it wasn't so hard missing out to him. I was glad to be his vice-captain. But Harvey was disappointed.

Not for the first time.

Two years earlier, he had missed out to Ian Craig.

'Bad luck, Nin. I thought you might have got it', said Craig.

Harvey assured him that he'd give his best under Craig's leadership.

And then, in 1961, at Lord's, he finally had his chance to lead the team.

Benaud was injured. As was Davidson.

The former completely ruled out and the latter almost out of it.

'I definitely cannot play tomorrow. There's no way I could see this Test out', lamented a distraught Davidson.

Benaud was clear in his mind: 'Alan, you have to play. I am out of the Test now and Neil needs you badly.'

5-42 from 24 overs.

All for his beloved Nin.

Harvey, the last of the Invincibles.

Neil Harvey was the most promising batsman in the early 1950s. Often regarded as one of the finest Australian batsmen in the immediate post-War years.

32 DON BRADMAN

King George V was not well in 1934 when the Australians visited England. At a dinner, Arthur Mailey was discussing cricket with Tom Clarke, the famous London journalist. Mailey asked Clarke if the Don and the king were to expire simultaneously, who would get the front page of the newspaper. Clarke was muted for a moment. He then suggested that both would be displayed on front page. The king would occupy the top left-hand side and Don the top right.

Jack Ingham, sports director of *The Star*, wrote in 1938: 'It is strange, but I think true, that all the time, day and night, somewhere in the world, someone is talking about Bradman.'

But the greatest compliment was surely given by Denzil Batchelor in his *Book of Cricket*: 'So quick were Bradman's reflexes that he was able to don his sweater while in the act of driving TPB Smith for four!'

One of Bradman's biographers, Roland Perry, once collected some rare video footage of the man in action from the British Film Archive. When he asked the Don if he wished to see them, he answered: 'I'm sick of Bradman.'

We aren't.

Needs no introduction.

33 WILFRED RHODES

1 August 1967.
Dean Park, Bournemouth.
Yorkshire v Hampshire.

A blind man was sitting near the boundary edge. He was relying on his hearing to picture the play.

Don Wilson and Geoff Cope, the Yorkshire spin twins, went to say hello to him.

'That man's too deep. Is he on the boundary edge?'

'It seems near... Why isn't he halfway?'

He went on and then said, 'I'm going to ask you a favour. They have asked me down to the local school where my grandchildren are. They have got a new cricket pitch and they want me to open it tomorrow morning. Will you come down?'

It was an artificial pitch.

This blind man said, 'I'll bowl the first ball.'

He touched the stumps, shuffled a bit and said, 'Am I about on the batting crease?'

Then he put his newspaper down on a length and went to the other end.

The ball bounced on the newspaper and went towards the slips.

Blind. Nearly 90.
But accurate.

No wonder Wilfred Rhodes took Test wickets even when he was 52.

Wilfred Rhodes' numbers suggest that there was never a greater all-round cricketer in the history of the game.

34 STEWIE DEMPSTER

February 1974.

David Frith, the editor of The Cricketer magazine, rings Ian Peebles and asks him to write an obituary.

Peebles declines, saying he disliked the man.

Peebles was not the only one.

This man wasn't the easiest to deal with. He had his own ways and he was rarely flexible enough to accommodate other people's views.

It all started really early, during a rather forgettable childhood.

He was very young when his father had to appear in court for stealing. His parents were in court at the same time fighting for divorce because his mother was having a relationship with the plumber.

Thankfully for him, there was cricket.

He liked playing it and did well whenever he got a chance to bat.

He was so good that Julien Cahn, the eccentric entrepreneur, appointed him as his store manager in Leicester so that he could captain the near-bankrupt county.

He was the finest against slow bowling in the 1930s.

And, according to Denzil Batchelor, no one could hit the ball harder through the offside.

But it was Stewie Dempster's private life that created more headlines.

He married thrice and had innumerable affairs.

Most of them made it to the newspapers, either in England or in New Zealand.

So much so that his biographer contemplated changing

the working title of the book from Second Only to Bradman to A Ladies Man.

Even Getty Images has captioned a picture of Dempster wrongly.

Dempster can be seen sitting on the customer's chair of his own little shop in Leicester.

The caption says that Dempster was the barber.

But he was New Zealand's first great batsman.

Once, as he approached a century at Lord's, a spectator shouted, 'Why wasn't I told about this before? Here is one of the most beautiful stroke-players I've ever seen and you critics have been hiding him all these years. You've wasted your adjectives on the hacks and here is a master.'

Stewie Dempster was the first great New Zealand batsman.

35 COLIN MCDONALD

The Australian Cricket Board didn't allow the families of cricketers to stay with them in England during the 1961 Ashes.

The manager and the captain were not the best of friends and there were divisions in the team management.

Colin McDonald decided to go against the board by keeping his family in England.

Alec Bedser arranged a hotel for them.

And a new car.

McDonald used it well. But he developed a sore wrist from changing the gears and was ruled out of the final two Tests of the series.

He never played again.

But, whenever asked, he did the job for his country.

According to Johnnie Moyes, McDonald faced the fastest ball he'd ever seen.

And it was he who made Fred Trueman use his nastiest expletives during the 1958–59 Ashes.

In the final innings of that series, Trueman reminded him: 'Ah think ah should tell thee ah'm on 99 Test wickets.'

'Well, Fred, I am on 468 runs for the series, so I'd like my 500th. And, anyway, you're a good enough bowler to get me out without me having to give it to you. Now piss off.'

Trueman took his 100th wicket in New Zealand.

McDonald was at his best when they came to India in 1959–60.

No, not with a bat in hand.

But as a peacemaker.

Australians weren't very happy with how things went outside the field of play.

Moreover, they thought, all the umpires were inefficient.

It was McDonald who kept them calm by lecturing all

through the tour: 'Come on fellas, be nice to these people. We're all diplomats on this tour.'

But even he got fed up during the final Test in Calcutta.

They had the Indian captain lbw twice, plumb, and he was given 'not out'.

Then Alan Davidson got him out bowled, with the off-stump uprooted.

McDonald came running from the fine-leg boundary and kicked the remaining two stumps before saying: 'That must have been bloody close!'

He is getting on in years, 90 at the time of writing.
Quite seriously ill.
But he wants to visit England. One last time.

Colin McDonald took the blows from the fastest of bowlers in the 1950s. An unsung hero of that Australian team.

36 KEPLER WESSELS

The 21-year-old was very happy with the 46 he scored against the likes of Garth le Roux, Derek Underwood, and Imran Khan. His smile evaporated as soon as he met Kerry Packer.

'Mate, I don't import people to get 40s.'

The smile was back after he scored a century in the next match. This time, even Packer was smiling.

After World Series Cricket ended, he wrote letters to some Australian cricketers he knew asking for suggestions regarding the state that he should join.

Rod Marsh's reply came first: 'Before you do anything, go and finish Grade 3 handwriting.'

His handwriting improved and so did his cricket.

But his greatest achievement — even greater than what some people may consider the epitome of modern-day achievement, coaching Chennai Super Kings — was fixing up Viv Richards in a match at the SCG.

This is what renowned cricket historian David Frith has to say about it:

'Richards kept turning to the wicketkeeper, Steve Rixon, and threatening to meet him after the game (i.e. to smash him: he often did this). Rixon was worried, but Wessels, who had been listening to this garbage at first slip, broke in to tell Richards that he was ready to take him on. That shut him up.'

It was known that Wessels (with his broken nose) had once been a serious boxer.

Kepler Wessels played international cricket for both Australia and South Africa (after they made a 'comeback' in the early 1990s). He was also a part of Kerry Packer's 'World Series Cricket'.

First-Class Greats

37 ALAN TOWNSEND

That was a bad Monday for the 13-year-old.

At half past five in the morning, he was woken by his mother.

'Your dad is going now. Do you still want to go?'

Leeds was 65 miles from their home in Middlesbrough, but cricket was his first love. He said yes.

Beef sandwiches for lunch. Tomato sandwiches for tea.

They mounted their bicycles.

His cycle had no gears.

They arrived at Headingley to find that play had already started. Bradman had resumed his innings. He was batting on 271, trying to go past Hammond's world record score of 336.

After six hours of cycling, there was no seat.

He had to stand all day.

Bradman could manage only 304. And then England lost four wickets in their second innings, staring at an innings defeat.

They were eventually saved by rain.

But for young Alan Townsend, it was the first flavour of top-level cricket.

It was a hot day and on the way home, they stopped for drinks. Alan had a bottle of lemonade.

It was nearly 8 o'clock and there were another 60 miles to go.

It was a lonely road. It rained badly and they got drenched.

At midnight, with 25 miles still to go, they found a fish and chips shop open.

The biggest problem was that the roads were lonely and

dark.

A 13-year-old cycling in that, with images of Bradman running through his mind.

They reached home well after 2 o'clock.

130 miles of cycling and standing all day in the heat.

But Bradman's drives and Cyril Walter's cuts were good enough to keep him going.

On that very day, he decided that life without cricket wouldn't be worthwhile.

He did well — played over 300 first-class matches for Warwickshire.

What if his mother had failed to wake him up that Monday?

Alan Townsend served Warwickshire for over a decade. He was a good batsman, decent bowler and brilliant catcher.

38 SAM COOK

A Worcestershire man recommended him to Gloucestershire.

He turned up for the pre-season nets, unknown and uncertain about the county ground protocol.

He recognised Wally Hammond and said: 'I'm Cook.'

The Master's eyed searched for more explanation.

Cook added: 'Cook—from Tetbury.'

He had to bowl to Hammond. He did well.

He earned the county cap at the end of the season.

The very next year, he was selected to play for England—a flat batting paradise at Trent Bridge.

Tom Goddard took him aside before the match: 'If you've got any sense, you want to call off sick while you have time.'

But Sam Cook never walked away from challenges.

Match figures of 30 4 127 0.

End of the Test career.

In those days, Charlie Barnett picked him up each morning on his way through Tetbury.

Then, near the end of 1948, Barnett retired.

So, Cook had to wait for the Bristol bus at seven each morning, then bowl 30 or 40 overs in a day.

At the end of the day, he hoped someone would respond to the message over the Tannoy: 'If anybody is going to Tetbury, Sam Cook would like a lift home.'

On many days, there was no response. He had to take a long bus journey and then walk five miles home.

All this, six days a week during the summer.

At the end of the cricket season, he became Tetbury's favourite plumber.

He was a good umpire as well. Apart from a short break

to look after his ailing wife, he did well for over two decades.

Towards the end of his life, he thought of writing a memoir.

He called it Bowling Down the Road.

He wrote a few pages and then realised that he was perhaps not important enough a man to write a memoir.

It remained unfinished.

Sam Cook bowled left-arm spin for Gloucestershire. And in one Test match for England. He later became an umpire.

39 DON WILSON

Bert Sutcliffe did it against Neil Adcock.

Geoff Edrich managed to do it against a rampaging Frank Tyson.

And 'Mad Jack' did it against 'Mad Jack'.

On Tuesday the sixth of June 1961, Worcestershire thought they had beaten Yorkshire, the defending champions, by 35 runs.

The crowd stood up on seeing the players preparing to leave the field.

Then Don Wilson came out. His left arm in plaster from elbow to knuckles.

The match was not over. One more wicket was to be taken.

Don was injured on Saturday and by Tuesday should have been back with the specialist in Leeds.

He had broken a bone at the base of his thumb.

His captain was furious when Don wanted to bat: 'You are not batting. You could do yourself incredible damage. If you bat, you'll never bat for Yorkshire again.'

They were 86 for 7, chasing 190 to win.

But then there was a 60-run partnership.

'All right. If there's just five minutes to go, you can bat.'

9 for 154 with half an hour to go. But no one could stop Don from going out.

He had to defend most of the balls—it was painful.

Then, with ten minutes to go, he swung away at two leg-side balls from Norman Gifford to bring the target down to 22.

Bob Platt, his partner, was astonished.

'What the hell are you doing? We are playing for a draw!'
'We're not. We are going for a win.'

'Mad Jack' Flavell was at his peak. He had taken 171 wickets in 1961 to earn a place in the England team.

Seeing him at the top of his run-up, Don was suggested to 'waste some time—adjust your box'.

But he was swinging with just one hand on the bat.

18 came of the over.

'Flavell let out more expletives in those few minutes than Fred Trueman got through in a whole season!'

Four to get. One over to be bowled.

'Just touch it. Let's get one', shouted Don.

He got the strike after scampering for a single.

And then a straight hit over Len Coldwell's head for four…

29 not out. Worth more than most centuries scored in first-class cricket.

In Yorkshire Post, Jim Kilburn wrote: 'The only possible finish that would serve the cause of romance…'

Don Wilson successfully succeeded Johnny Wardle and went on to take over 1000 wickets for Yorkshire.

But if anything defined the way he played the game, it was that innings of 29 not out on a warm evening at New Road.

Don Wilson was a part of the dominant Yorkshire team of the 1960s. He later became MCC's chief coach.

40 TOM CARTWRIGHT

As a young car worker in Coventry, Tom Cartwright loved listening to the political talks in the tea breaks, when they all sat round and put the world to rights.

Then, he became a cricketer—a very good one who learnt his game in the days of uncovered pitches and three-day county cricket. In those bygone days, television and commercial sponsors didn't influence the game.

When cricket, in Tom's words, was 'the people's summer game'.

He still loved listening to the senior cricketers. He hardly spoke in those days.

Then, as the years went by, Tom changed from a listener to a speaker.

Everyone who knew him agreed on one thing: he knew a great deal about cricket, more than anyone they had ever met.

He always thought that it was his duty to serve the game—in any way possible.

When Stephen Chalke wanted to write a book on him, he said yes.

At the age of 70, he used to happily drive from Neath to Cardiff for regular lunchtime meetings with his biographer.

He was always concerned about the wellbeing of the game.

'Not many people want to take up issues, you know. They don't. They really don't. Sometimes I wish I could walk away, but I can't.'

A week before the release of his life-story, he rung up Chalke to say that his wife's best friend, a retired head teacher, had read the book and had called to tell him how good it was. 'It's not easy to write that well', she told him, and he wanted to pass the compliment on to the author.

Later that day, he collapsed. It was a major heart attack. He never recovered.

For once, he had to walk away from seeing his life-story winning awards.

Tom Cartwright served Warwickshire for many years and then became a successful coach.

41 ROBIN HOBBS

7 for 227 in the fourth innings while chasing 325 for victory.

The number four batsman is doing it all alone. He is well past his century.

The number nine batsman, in his final first-class appearance, joins him in the middle.

Together, they add a vital 43 runs in 12 overs. The number nine batsman's contribution is a duck, out to the first ball he faces for six overs.

They eventually lose the match by 13 runs.

Javed Miandad's unbeaten 200 proves to be not enough.

That Miandad innings is now part of Glamorgan cricket folklore.

But that number nine batsman is largely forgotten. His dogged resistance with the bat is not remembered. Nor does anyone remember his five-wicket haul in that match.

Robin Hobbs is a forgotten cricketer. A leg-spin bowler who played for England after the Second World War.

He was a brilliant fielder at cover point.

He once scored a century in 44 minutes against the touring Australian team.

One of my favourite cricket stories involves two spinners. One of them is Hobbs.

No batsman has a higher average on one ground than Yorkshire's Geoff Boycott at the Garrison Ground in Colchester.

In 1971, he ended the first day on 221 not out.

Next morning he, as captain of the team, chose to continue batting. But 25 minutes into the session, he was dismissed lbw to Robin Hobbs.

Umpire Sam Cook (the other spinner in the story) had no hesitation in raising his finger.

Boycott was already running the leg bye and he turned to Cook and said, 'No, no, no, Sam, that can't be lbw.'

'That's out.', said Cook, and then turned to Hobbs and added, 'I think we have seen enough of him.'

'It was not out. Everyone knew that', is what Hobbs now says.

Robin Hobbs has a fund of such stories. But he never shared them with the public.

Finally, first-time writer Rob Kelly has managed to convince him. Stephen Chalke has recommended Patrick Ferriday's name to Kelly, with Ferriday as publisher, the book on Robin Hobbs was ready.

It was eventually published in May 2018.

Robin Hobbs represents that rare breed: an English leg spinner.

42 BILL COPSON

No team won the county championship in the inter-War period without their fast bowlers.

Lancashire had Macdonald and Pollard (later), Yorkshire had Waddington and Bowes, Nottinghamshire had Larwood and Voce, and Middlesex had Durston.

A group of miners won the championship in 1936. They had Bill Copson.

The yearly earning of the average miner in the 1930s was less than 150 GBP, whereas for a decent county cricketer it was approximately 300 GBP.

So, while there was always an urge to play the game, the opportunities were missing.

Copson attended a school for some years but there was no facility to play cricket there.

At the age of 14, rather reluctantly, he found his way into the pit.

In 1926, during the General Strike, he was working in the Morton Colliery.

There was a local playground where the miners used to play some cricket and Copson too joined them that year.

It was there that Morton's secretary discovered him.

In 1931, Derbyshire wanted to test the youngster. He did well and when he got a chance to prove himself the very next year. He took the wicket of Andy Sandham—Test cricket's first triple centurion—with his first ball in first-class cricket.

There was no looking back from that point.

The only problem was that he was injury-prone and not the healthiest of cricketers.

In 1935–36, to remain fit, he trained with the Chesterfield FC first team and when the cricket season commenced in 1936, he was at his best.

Copson and Mitchell.
In A.A. Thomson's words, 'brimstone and treacle'.
They made the miners believe that they could do it. And they did it.

'Whistle down a pit in Derbyshire and up comes a fast bowler'.
Yes, there were many of them but it was the emergence of Copson which gave rise to this legend.

If he were healthier and if there had been no Second World War, he could easily have become one of the very best in the history of England's cricket.

Bill Copson was the prime architect of one of the most extraordinary triumphs in the history of cricket.

Derbyshire's coal mines have produced many notable fast bowlers. Bill Copson's name should be there in the top three.

43 ROY MARSHALL

Nelson v Lowerhouse at Seedhill in 1952.

A match that proved to be important for cricket in England.

Lancashire League, in those days, had this system of collections for bowlers who took six wickets in an innings and for batsmen who scored 50 or more.

Ray Lindwall, bowling at his best, took the first six wickets of Lowerhouse for next to nothing.

The Lowerhouse opener had to see all of that from the non-striker's end.

He was 14 short of his half-century.

'Have a heart, Ray. You've made sure of your collection. I want to live, how about letting me get mine?'

Lindwall replied: 'Okay.'

He bowled a few balls way outside the off-stump and allowed the batsman at the other end to reach his half-century. In the process, Lindwall lost his rhythm and the match ended in a draw.

Soon after this match, that batsman was invited to join Hampshire.

Ray Marshall had already played four Test matches for West Indies and, according to many, was as good as Clyde Walcott.

He brought life back into county cricket.

At a time when the likes of Geoff Boycott and Bill Lawry bored people, Test cricket needed Marshall. But it was not to be. By joining Hampshire after playing Tests for West Indies, he lost his chance of playing for either country.

It was he who questioned everything that was rigid in the

county circuit. Colin Ingleby-Mackenzie benefitted from his ideas and gave birth to the triumphant 'wine, women, and song' Hampshire team of 1961.

Roy Marshall could bat. He was a tremendous attacking batsman. Bowlers used to have sleepless nights before bowling to him.
And all this before the likes of Virender Sehwag and Matthew Hayden were born.

Roy Marshall, a West Indian, played most of his cricket for Hampshire. He was a very successful and respected batsman in county cricket.

44 ALLAN WATKINS

The Lindwall bouncer hit him on the shoulder. Unable to recover from the blow, he could get his feet nowhere against a Johnston delivery that swung in the air and was dismissed for a duck.

He came back to the dressing room to discover that the shoulder was all black and blue.

He was strapped up but that didn't have any effect on his captain.

'What do you think the bloody skipper did? He only gave me the new ball to bowl!'

Four expensive overs and the ever-increasing pain made sure that he was off the field.

He came back on the field an hour later and was told to take his position at short leg against the leg-spinner.

A bit too much for a debutant!

But then, as the first wicket went down, everyone stood up to applaud the incoming batsman. It was a moment to savour.

The new batsman defended the first ball to be picked up by this hapless debutant.

Then, on the next ball, the batsman was dismissed bowled.

Bradman b Hollies 0.

'He had the shock of his life when it bowled him! He looked down very quickly to see what the hell had happened.'

Had emotion finally got the better of the world's greatest run-maker?

'I don't know, I can't say that', he replied, 'but I can tell you he was dry-eyed!'

Albert Watkins was an ordinary student who preferred being out playing games all through the year.

He made his first-class debut as a 17-year-old.

Some people wanted his autograph and to one of them, he casually said, 'I wish I had a shorter name.'

'Why don't you sign as Alan?', suggested Wilf Wooller.

He signed 'Allan' and that's the name the press used while writing about his exploits.

The war was not the best of times for Allan, and his cricket suffered badly.

As soon as the war was over, he resumed his career as a baker and thought of quitting cricket.

The news reached his former headmaster at school, who, at one point, had been critical about Allan's studies and his future.

He wrote to his former pupil, reminding him of the sacrifices his parents had made to help with the cost of kit and fares for him to reach the matches.

Allan went back to playing cricket.

He did rather well for Glamorgan and decently for England as well.

'It was a strenuous life', he admitted. 'But, as a youngster, it was what I had always dreamt of doing, sport, and that's what I've done. It made me take a lot of pills for being nervous, but I wouldn't change a minute.'

One of those who gave all they had to the game they loved yet found no one asking them for interviews or writing glowing pieces on them.

Allan Watkins was a regular in the Glamorgan team for close to two decades after the Second World War. He played 15 Tests for England.

45 ARTHUR WELLARD

Umpire Alec Skelding walked back from the pavilion to the middle at Wells, wagged a finger in mock rebuke at the batsman and said: 'For heaven's sake, don't lose this ball. We've run out of them!'

Frank Woolley, in his last season for Kent, was bowling. He had been hit for 5 sixes in a row. Several balls had disappeared far out of the ground and all of a sudden, there was an embarrassing shortage of replacements.

But the batsman dutifully restrained himself and settled for a few fours after that.

Then, he took 13 wickets and made sure that they won the match.

Arthur Wellard, born on 8 April 1902, should have, by rights, played for Kent. But they let him slip away. Somerset benefited from this and Wellard served them for close to 20 seasons.

Before the war, his out-swingers were effective and, notwithstanding the ordinary slip cordon of Somerset, fetched him plenty of wickets.

After the war, his limbs ached more and he turned to off-spin.

He was a magnificent fielder who often loitered at silly mid-off. He took catches as if he was pulling an ace from a pack. The ball was often in his pocket as puzzled spectators searched for it near the extra-cover boundary.

It was his big hitting that always grabbed attention. He scored roughly one-fourth of those 12,000-odd runs in sixes. He had a routine of defending the first half-dozen balls he faced and then issuing himself the license to go at everything thrown at him.

But he was at his best while playing poker. There was no one, absolutely no one, who could beat him at that.

In his book *Hit for Six*, Gerald Brodribb reserved several pages to flesh out Wellard's exploits.

Thirty-five years later, a Somerset fan named Barry Phillips got inspired by Brodribb's account and decided to write a biography of Wellard.

It was titled No Mere Slogger, a phrase first used by E.W. Swanton to describe Wellard's explosive batting.

In 2007, David Foot wrote on him as part of the series My Favourite Cricketer in The Wisden Cricketer.

According to Foot, Wellard was an uncomplicated man who enjoyed playing cricket.

When it rained, he would produce a pack of cards. In the words of Bill Andrews: 'He could remember the position of every card in the pack—he once again showed that he was out of our class.'

Arthur Wellard was a legend in Somerset cricket. His clean hitting made him a very popular figure in the West country.

46 LES JACKSON

In the 1950s, Hampshire used to have their northern tour with away-matches against Yorkshire, Lancashire, and Derbyshire.

In one of those years, Fred Trueman found Hampshire opener Jimmy Gray in a bar and asked him how he was enjoying the trip.

'Enjoying? First, I've got to face you at Park Avenue, then it's Brian Statham at Old Trafford, and as if it's not enough, there's that mean bastard Jackson at Burton-on-Trent… and you ask me if I'm enjoying it!'

Trueman used to call him 'the great F.S.' (after the other famous Jackson) and had no doubt that he was the best six-days-a-week bowler he had ever seen.

Jackson played two Test matches, 12 years apart.

The Australians could not believe when he was not selected for any of the Tests during the 1948 Ashes series.

In 1950–51, Gubby Allen thought that his arm was too low to be a success in Australia—perhaps the stupidest theory ever heard.

He could perhaps have played more if he was from another county like Surrey, Yorkshire, or Lancashire.

But instead, he was a miner (the only county cricketer to have worked in the mines post-World War II) and represented the unfashionable Derbyshire.

But he never regretted anything. He always gave his best and had his best season when he was 38.

Les Jackson remains one of the unluckiest bowlers in the history of Test cricket.

Little known trivia: The record for most dismissals by a fast bowler/keeper combination in FC cricket belongs to Les Jackson and George Dawkes (254).

Les Jackson was one of the best bowlers in county cricket.

47 HANUMANT SINGH

In 2006, Hanumant Singh died of dengue fever and hepatitis. He was cremated with a bat on his chest.

Hanumant's love for the game of cricket was well-known. He was an attractive batsman who didn't do full justice to his talent.

He was 24 when he played in the Indian Board President's XI v India Prime Minister's XI match in Bombay.

He scored 201 runs in that match. For a brief while, he batted with Australian legend Arthur Morris.

All this is well-known.

When Morris died, there was not even one Baggy Green in his possession.

The 2008 book on the Baggy Green, written by Michael Fahey and Mike Coward, clearly stated that Morris had three Baggy Greens.

He had happily given one to Frank Worrell and swapped another with Eric Hollies.

He had handed over the remaining one to a young Indian batsman who had turned his head in Bombay.

But Morris failed to recall his name.

Clayton Murzello, Sports Editor of *Mid-Day*, recently found a copy of Sport and Pastime, dated 1 October 1966.

As soon as he saw the magazine, with Hanumant adorned on its cover, it became clear to him who the lucky Indian batsman was.

Hanumant's son Sangram Singh later told him: 'I have the Baggy Green with me! My dad didn't let me wear it—even to try it on. He said stuff like this had to be earned! I think he never wore it himself. He just treasured it.'

Hanumant Singh played 14 Test matches for India in the 1960s.

48 ARTHUR MILTON

'No paradise lost for this Milton' was the headline of Frank Keating's portrait of Arthur Milton in *The Guardian*. A picture of Milton on a post office bicycle, delivering the mail around streets of Bristol, accompanied the article.

'He is in the sorting office by ten past five, gets his bundle into street order, then whistles off to the Downs of Clifton in cycle-clips…and no, he doesn't think much, anymore, of his previous incarnation on the foreign fields of fame.'

He was good at mathematics. He was on the verge of filling out forms for Oxford. And then, a scout from Arsenal arrived.

'I loved sport—and, when you're young, you don't think about getting old, do you?'

He played football for England at Wembley, in front of 100,000 people. He won a medal as part of Arsenal's championship winning side of 1952–53.

He opened the batting for England at Lord's and when he retired, no one barring the great Wally Hammond had scored more first-class runs for Gloucestershire.

Decades later, people often asked him one question: 'Do you realise if you were young today, with your looks and your sporting talent, you'd be a millionaire?'

He always smiled and replied: 'I've been married for fifty years. I've got three great boys, they've all done well, and I've got grandchildren too now. All my life I've had good health, and I was lucky enough to play the games I loved for a living. Out in the sunshine all summer. Then there were the years in the Post Office. Wonderful years, I learned so much from them. Now I'm up on the Downs each morning, watching the sun come up and the mist rising from the dew on the ground. There's nowhere I'd rather be.'

Then, after a brief pause, he never forgot to add: 'I am a millionaire.'

Arthur Milton was a talented sportsman who went on to become a double-international.

49 JIMMY BINKS

We seem to think that cricketers playing continuously for months is a modern-day phenomenon. And hence all of them deserve 'rest' during the not-so-important series or tournaments.

Jimmy Binks' extraordinary career is enough to debunk that myth. Binks, before his final season, missed ONE match in 13 years. In most of those years, he played cricket six days a week, continuously for five months.

He played a total of 77 matches in 1960 and 1961, in ten months' time.

Binks' father was a wicket-keeper in minor cricket. He knew how tough it could be. He always wanted his son to become a cricketer but not a wicket-keeper.

Binks, on the other hand, worshipped his father. He began keeping wicket at the age of 12.

Seven years later, he was summoned by Yorkshire's first team. He was paid on a match-by-match basis for two seasons.

And then Yorkshire decided to make him a permanent name in the team list.

That was the last great decision they took before deciding to sign Craig McDermott in 1992.

Despite all the talent and guidance, Binks' career could have ended when he was 18. A year before making his debut for Yorkshire, he was, like his future teammate Bob Appleyard, diagnosed with tuberculosis. He had to spend a good part of the year in hospital before he could resume playing.

Bob Appleyard found a Stephen Chalke to tell his story to the world.

Who'll do that for Jimmy Binks?

Jimmy Binks was the reliable Yorkshire wicketkeeper during their glory years in the 1960s.

50 TOM DOLLERY

'Drinks?

'What do you want drinks for? In the desert we had two pints of water a day—and that was for you and your vehicle.'

He had directed fire from artillery observation posts. He knew what it was to be fighting in a war.

He knew how life could end in a split second. He has seen it all.

Tom Dollery was a leader.

Old Warwickshire supporters still remember how the team marched out to the field of play.

Led by a man with a stern face, with some Brylcreem on his hair.

Dollery was not one to fuss over his appearance.

If he saw players spending time in front of a mirror, he gave them a terrible stick.

Once, during his early years, when the groundsman used a flame thrower to dry the pitch, Dollery persuaded his captain to send out tail-enders to start their second innings.

They scored some runs and helped Warwickshire win the match.

A few years later, Dollery was appointed the captain of the team.

A professional captain, he led a team in which there were no amateurs.

These were players with limited capability but they were ready to give their best under Dollery.

Then, in 1951, under Dollery, Warwickshire won the county championship.

The Times commented: '... and above all the popularity,

the skill and the knowledge of Dollery's captaincy. The whole side have pulled together with him and for him.'

He knew he was on trial.

Professional captaincy was an experiment and its future depended a lot on how Dollery and his men did.

Dollery was successful.

And he had a telling impact on the history of the game.

Next June, England were led onto the field by a professional named Len Hutton.

Tom Dollery, a professional, led Warwickshire to County Championship glory in 1951.

51 TOMMY GREENHOUGH

'The wickets are being covered next year. You'll be in the side from the start.'

Cyril Washbrook knew how to retain an important 'employee', even in 1958.

But he was as good as his word.

The leg-spinner bowled 300 overs in the first four weeks and got a call to play for England.

And then, at Lord's, as India were comfortably placed at 144 for 3, this leg-spinner struck.

Five times in the space of 31 balls.

Despite Godfrey Evans missing four stumping opportunities.

The Times wrote: 'His career will be full of blue skies.'

It never was.

1948.

Manchester United finally manages to win a major trophy, after a gap of 37 years.

The first stored-program computer is unveiled in Manchester.

And before all that, the Lancashire bowlers are able to stop the Bradman run-machine.

Meanwhile, a 16-year-old shop assistant with the Co-op is spotted and asked to appear for a trial in the Old Trafford nets.

'What do you bowl, lad?'

'I bowl off-breaks, leg-breaks, and googlies.'

'You can set a field for all of them. Anyway, I don't want to see you bowl off-spinners. They're ten a penny.'

He bowled leg-breaks all day. And got selected on the Lancashire staff.

1949 was a good year for Tommy Greenhough.

He got plenty of wickets bowling for the second eleven. He knew he was ready to make his first-class debut in 1950.

Then, in January that year, he fell 40 feet and shattered the metatarsals in both feet.

That, everyone thought, was the end of a promising leg-spinner.

Not to be.

He recovered and signed a contract in which he was paid week-to-week in 1951.

Greenhough played for 15 seasons.

With a misshapen right foot and against all odds.

That 5/35 against India at Lord's is still the best bowling figures by an English leg-spinner in the last 60 years.

Tommy Greenhough served Lancashire for a decade. An English le-break bowler who went on to play four Test matches.

The Unlucky XI

52 DUNCAN SHARPE

'You should pick him with your eyes shut'

Lala Amarnath had a glimpse of the youngster and had no hesitation in saying this to Fazal Mahmood.

Fazal was already impressed.

Earlier that year, he had driven from Blackburn to Stroud to watch him in a two-day match against Gloucestershire.

The young man scored a quick-fire half-century and Fazal's eyes lit up.

He took him aside and said: 'The Australians are coming. How do you feel about taking on Meckiff and Lindwall and Benaud?'

He quietly answered that he could face anybody.

Fazal smiled and said: 'That's what I wanted to hear.'

Long back, this young man had spent many a day and night dreaming about facing Ray Lindwall.

It was about to come true.

He was the third Christian to play for Pakistan.

In his debut Test against Australia, he used bats and boots borrowed from the first of the two—Wallis Mathias.

He did alright in the three Test matches but was not invited to play against India in the next series.

Duncan Sharpe could have been a film star from the 1950s. He was often mistaken for Cary Grant.

Just before he managed to break through to the Pakistan team, he got married. It was short-lived. He had an infant son who never saw his father.

45 years later, his granddaughter discovered him through an internet search.

By then, Sharpe was settled in Australia.

He left for Australia after he had failed to make it to the team for India.

He and his girlfriend Gillian both had British passports (according to his Pakistan teammates, she could easily put Elizabeth Taylor in the shade).

Barry Jarman did the rest.

. Sharpe migrated to Australia and began playing in the Sheffield Shield.

His stroke-play was often breath-taking and it impressed Bradman, who secured him a job of assisting the curator at the Adelaide Oval.

Duncan Sharpe did well.

Shook hands with a U.S. president.

Got Bradman clapping for him.

Scored more runs than Sobers in a century partnership.

Scored all the runs in a partnership with Ian Chappell, who just watched him with awe from the other end.

But he is largely forgotten.

Other than by quizmasters, who make questions like:

Complete the list: 'Wallis Mathias, Antao D' Souza, Duncan Sharpe, ________.'

Duncan Sharpe, an Anglo-Pakistani, was an attacking batsman who deserved to play more than the three Test matches he played.

53 JACK IVERSON

He never gave the photographers enough time to click a picture of him batting.

According to one of his opponents, he carried his bat 'like a businessman carrying his newspaper to work on a tram'.

He was a fast bowler for the college second XI team.

He was an ordinary bowler and was more interested in golf.

He joined his father's real-estate business before the war broke out.

The war was bad, but it did help him get back to cricket.

He was back playing cricket regularly but the heat was too much for him and he switched to bowling the 'specials' he had by then developed.

He wasn't successful and, after the war, went back to his father's business.

One day, he and his wife were strolling through a park.

There he saw some blind cricketers in action.

That was enough.

He went back to cricket once again and this time he tasted success.

Not as a batsman. Not as a fast bowler.

But by bowling those 'specials'.

Jack Iverson was the star of the 1950–51 Ashes series. English batsmen struggled against his mysterious bowling.

54 JACK MACBRYAN

His father, he vehemently believed, had little love for him and chose to obstruct his professional career.

He wanted to be a doctor specialising in neurology and mental disorders.

His father, who ran a mental asylum, did all he could to prevent his son from becoming a doctor.

After he was taken prisoner in the First World War, there was a chance of an exchange repatriation involving him and a German doctor.

His father did nothing about it.

He was close to his mother, who died when he was young.

His favourite brother died in the war.

His marriage was a disaster. The girl soon fancied someone else and left home with him.

And then, through no fault of his own, he lost all he had on the Stock Exchange.

This is the story of Jack MacBryan. He wanted to play for Middlesex but had to be content playing for Somerset, with a bunch of 'terrible amateurs'.

He played a Test match in which he didn't get a chance to bat.

But he was lucky.

South Africa's Bevil Rudd won the 400-meter event in the 1920 Olympic Games.

But most of the British competitors were ushered off home as soon as their events were over.

MacBryan was still there (as part of the British Hockey team), however, at the time of the prize-giving by the King of Belgium.

He was asked to take Rudd's place.

He is the only Test cricketer to receive an Olympic gold medal in athletics.

Jack MacBryan was a leading Somerset cricketer in the immediate Post World War I years. He played one Test match but didn't get the chance to bat or bowl.

55 SHANE BOND

July 2001.

NZ Cricket High Performance Centre, Lincoln.

Richard Hadlee has the rather difficult task of selecting a replacement for the injured Scott Styris, who was supposed to fly to India to play for the NZ A team in the Buchi Babu Tournament in Chennai.

Dayle Hadlee, the Academy director, has no hesitation in his mind.

As soon as he meets his brother, he smiles and says: 'Your replacement is in the nets now— it's Shane Bond.'

Bond, after getting approval and leave from the police force, plays in the tournament and makes most Indian batsmen look clueless against him.

Back home, Hadlee faces criticism for selecting Bond. One even writes: 'The worst selection decision ever made by the national selectors.'

Later that year, as soon as Shayne O'Connor and Dion Nash breaks down in Australia, Hadlee summons Bond.

He impresses everyone in the very first Test he plays.

At the end of the first day, Hadlee and his wife visit a restaurant near their hotel. The manager apologises and says they must wait for an hour to get a table.

Enter Shane Bond and family.

'Any chance of getting a table for four without booking?'

'Certainly Mr Bond. It's my pleasure. Please come this way.'

Bond invites the Hadlees to join them.

'A table for six, please?'

'Certainly, Mr Bond.'

Injury-prone but when fit, there was none better than him.

Shane Bond, at his best, was almost impossible to face. Unfortunately, his career was plagued with injuries.

56 JOHN BENAUD

5, Sutherland Road, North Parramatta.

The elder son is back home from his first tour of England and announces that he will be cooking dinner that night.

The younger one, nine years old, is very happy to get his brother back but a bit worried on hearing his brother's announcement.

He cooks Hungarian Goulash, an international dish about which he came to know in England, but it ends up a disaster. His mother somehow manages to salvage the situation.

In-com-pre-hens-ible, shouts the elder one as he eats 'Hungarian Goulash'.

The younger one tries to console him. He borrows what his brother always tells him: 'Never take yourself too seriously.'

Four years earlier, they used to walk together to the little red phone box at the top of Sutherland Road and then the elder brother always called one of his friends and at some point uttered, 'in-com-pre-hens-ible'.

That's the first word the young boy learnt from his big brother. Many more were to follow.

A few years later, he took him to the SCG to give him a flavour of Test match cricket.

'Typhoon' Tyson created havoc as Australia lost. The ten-year-old was thrilled to see his brother dismiss a young promising batsman named Colin Cowdrey.

Sixteen years later, when the younger brother made his Test debut, the older one was present there as a journalist.

He had only one advice for him: 'Never take yourself too seriously.'

John Benaud never took himself too seriously.

He lost the captaincy and his place in the New South Wales team only because of his insistence upon sticking to a certain brand of footwear.

But he always enjoyed playing the game.

He was always proud to have Richie as his brother.

He was the one who first came up with the 'You've just dropped the World Cup' bit in 1999. Frank Keating repeated the same thing the next day and it became famous.

No one knew who started it.

Very few know there's another Benaud who did decently while playing the game he loved.

Frank 'Typhoon' Tyson played a key role in England's triumph in the 1954–55 Ashes series.

John Benaud, a keen and passionate cricketer, has always been overshadowed by his more famous elder brother Richie.

57 ISRAR ALI

April 1959.

A flat in East Lancashire.

The captain of the Bacup team had come to meet Fazal Mahmood, Hanif Mohammad, and Israr Ali.

Fazal offered him Hanif—a world-class batsman—but they didn't want him. They thought that Hanif was too slow and only fit to bat out for draws.

'We want Israr.'

They offered £700 per season. Israr asked for 1,000 GBP. Fazal suggested £900. Then they all agreed on £800 for a year.

In that summer of 1959, Israr scored close to 1,000 runs, averaging over 50.

He took 47 wickets at 22.

And dismissed a bloke named Garry Sobers. Clean bowled.

They were impressed and wanted to give him a contract for the next two seasons.

Despite his differences with supremo A.H. Kardar, Israr was recalled to the Test team for the home series against Australia.

It all looked good—until a bus accident later that winter ended his cricket career.

Most of the people travelling in that bus were killed. Israr survived after a five-hour long operation by Lahore's best surgeon.

His career ended and, rather ironically, he started his own transport business.

He had seen the worst of the partition in 1947.
He had also seen the worst of A.H. Kardar.

And then there was that life-threatening accident.

But, Israr Ali was very proud to have represented Pakistan in Test cricket.

A.H. Kardar was the supremo of Pakistan cricket in their early years of cricket. Fazal Mahmood and Hanif Mohammad were the two most famous cricketers in the Pakistan team in their first two decades in international cricket.

Israr Ali was not that great a cricketer but he enjoyed his time and gave his all on the field of play.

58 MIRAN BUX

A few days ago, while thinking about how unlucky Les Jackson was, I tried to think of some of the luckiest Test cricketers who had no influence on their own selection (leaving out the notorious Vizzy and a few others like that).

The first name I could think of holds the record for the oldest debutant in the 20th century.

Miran Bux studied till the eighth standard and then became a sepoy in the Army.

He was a good cricketer and often played in teams dominated by British people.

But then, he would never have played Test cricket.

He bowled seven economical overs in a first-class match and then disappeared from the first-class game.

Pakistan toured India and England but Bux was nowhere close to being selected.

So why was then he selected, all of a sudden, as a 47-year-old off-spinner, in a Test against India in 1955?

The reason was related to A.H. Kardar's family matters.

When Pakistan needed a third spinner, they had their first choice ready—Zulfiqar Ahmed. He was 20 years younger than Bux and had a better FC record.

But he was Kardar's brother-in-law and had opposed Kardar's second marriage to an English lady.

The rift kept him out of the Tests against India.

Enter Miran Bux.

He knew no one in the team. His cricket kit was different from others. He didn't have a green Pakistan blazer.

Two Test matches. One run. Two wickets.

That was it for the veteran.

Thirty years later, he got a benefit match and earned Rs 125,000.

Then, in February 1991, while out for a morning walk, he died near his house. No one recognised him. Loudspeakers at the nearby mosques announced that the dead body of an unknown man had been found.

Miran Bux, quite miraculously, played Test cricket, and even has quiz questions asked on him.

Miran Bux's main claim to fame is that he was the second oldest debutant in Test history.

59 JIMMY MATTHEWS

The tales of the likes of Billy Bates, Drewy Stoddart, Billy Midwinter etc. are well known.

Jimmy Matthews is also well-known but, rather thankfully, not for his tragic life.

Averse to the English weather, he declined offers from several counties.

But he had to go back to Europe during the war. It was a horrific experience for him—his brother-in-law died in front of him.

Thankfully, his gastric ulcer became unbearable and he was eventually repatriated.

The war ended but he failed to make a comeback. Misfortune was never too far away from him. Even before the war, an injury at the wrong time and an undue investigation by the Australian board at the end of the American leg of the 1912 tour conspired against him.

He continued to play cricket till the mid-1930s. It was cricket that somehow prevented him from falling into the grasp of acute depression.

The depression years were terrible. Tuberculosis and other industrial respiratory diseases devastated families. No family suffered more than his. He lost his wife and five of their nine children.

It is almost impossible to comprehend how tragic and soul-destroying it must have been.

But playing cricket always rescued him from these setbacks.

The gastric ulcer was recurring all too often, but every time everyone thought that his career was over, he stunned them by making another comeback.

He passed away in October 1943. The cause of death was pulmonary tuberculosis which, according to his death certificate, he had battled with for years.

Thirty-one years before all that, he created history by taking two hat-tricks in a Test match.

Jimmy Matthews is a name that every quizzer is familiar with, but not many know that his greatest achievement was the way he kept playing the game despite suffering setbacks of the worst kind.

Jimmy Matthews is still the only cricketer to take two hat-tricks in a Test match.

60 HAROLD GIMBLETT

22 May 1976.

Gloucestershire v Leicestershire in the Benson & Hedges Cup.

The match was well on its way, but the adjudicator was missing.

It was a certain Harold Gimblett.

He could finally be spotted in the late afternoon. David Foot walked up to him. Gimblett put an arm around Foot's shoulder.

'Thank God someone will talk to me.'

A few months later he phoned Foot one evening. Would he help him write a book?

'I don't want it to be like any of the other cricket books. I want the public to know what it is really like being a professional sportsman, when you're a worrier. The mental battles for me have been enormous and maybe it would be a good idea to put it on record.'

He then bought a small cassette recorder to record his thoughts.

'I'm doing it in the middle of the night when I can't sleep... It's going to be very personal.'

He died in 1978.

The final cassette, handed over to Foot by Mrs Gimblett a few months after her husband's death, started thus:

'David, this is my attempt at a possible book. The only thing I'm absolutely certain of is the title. At the ripe old age of 63, I feel the title must be *No More Bouncers*...not that I was ever afraid of 'em...'

He wasn't. On good days, he could score at will against

anyone.

On bad days, he didn't bother to think of ways to make runs. Those were bad days.

Gimblett was moody but, again on good days, could be a gem of a person.

Ken Biddulph knew it.

29 April 1954.

Somerset v Hampshire friendly at Taunton.

Biddulph had just got a six-month contract. He didn't know what would happen after six months and whether it was at all worth leaving his day job.

Gimblett was getting ready to go out to bat. Biddulph knocked on the door.

'Come in… what can I do for you?'

'I wonder if I could have a word with you after close of play, Mr Gimblett?'

'Never mind the close of play. Come in and sit down.'

'But they'll be waiting for you.'

'Let them wait. You're more important at the moment. What's on your mind?'

Biddulph told him about the offer.

'You can go back in and tell that stupid secretary of ours to shove it up his arse.'

'I can't do that!'

'No, I suppose you can't. I'll tell him…'

Then he strode out and scored 97 in no time.

A few days later, Biddulph got a two-year contract.

The tormented genius.

Harold Gimblett was a Somerset legend. He played three Test matches for England.

61 COLIN MILBURN

The 11th ball in his comeback match.

Going through the defences of an international cricketer.

Racing to congratulate him, his jubilant teammates found him on all fours on the turf.

He was frantically searching for his glass eye, which he eventually found halfway down the wicket.

It was a good comeback but everyone knew how tough the task was.

It was close to four years that a tragic accident had affected his eyes.

He had given all his kit away. He only played squash with former teammate Alan Hodgson.

Hodgson realised that the 'eye' was still working fine and persuaded him to start training with the second XI.

And then, injuries to a couple of first-team regulars opened the door for him.

But he struggled.

Anyone would have, without the leading eye and with only 80% visibility in the other eye.

But there was the odd flash of brilliance.

He scored a 50 against Surrey.

He swept Robin Jackman to the groundsman's garden.

Everyone was filled with hope.

But it was not to be .

Colin Milburn loved the drum and guitar beats. He used to relax listening to that kind of music.

Then the accident happened.

Once David Frith gave him a lift in his car and played a tape that he thought would grab him for its strong drum and guitar beat—but he just murmured 'All right, I suppose.'

It was not to be…

As great a tragedy as cricket has known.

Colin Milburn was touted as the next best thing in English cricket. An unfortunate accident ended it all rather abruptly.

62 FRED BAKEWELL

'He's something of a wandering minstrel and a sad case.'

He was not to be found easily. Some even thought that he was dead.

But Ken Turner, the Northants secretary, tracked him down.

David Frith drove to St Albans to record the story.

It wasn't a happy one.

The 'agricultural college' where Fred Bakewell spent some time as a youth was Borstal!

Then, he got a chance to show his cricketing skills.

The game rescued him.

He was the batting mainstay of a team that won 18 games out of 250 in a decade's time.

In 1936, without a win all summer, at Chesterfield, they faced the new champions—Derbyshire.

Bakewell scored a brilliant 241 not out in their second innings.

It was an innings worth celebrating. He duly did it with 'four or five beers'.

And then climbed into the passenger seat of the teetotaller Reggie Northway.

Their teammate Jack Timms knew the road and these two decided to follow him.

Bakewell was tired and fell into a deep sleep.

When he woke, he found himself in hospital.

Northway was no longer alive.

Had Northway fallen asleep at the wheel?

Or was he driving too fast for a dark, empty road?

Bakewell survived but he never played another serious cricket match.

In the 1960s, he suffered another accident and lost an eye.

But the real damage was done in 1936.

The man who could have succeeded Herbert Sutcliffe and was capable of 'batting with Bradman on not uneven terms' had to call it a day at 27.

Fred Bakewell played for Northamptonshire in the 1930s. He was a world-class performer in a rather ordinary team.

The Swashbucklers

63 JOHNNY DOUGLAS

JWHT Douglas is better known than many cricketers who did better than him. He is a trivia hunter's delight.

The Australian public 'lovingly' called him 'Johnny Won't Hit Today' Douglas. He was a boxer—an Olympic champion. Decades later, he was drowned at sea trying to save his father's life.

But my favourite JWHT story is little-known, perhaps because it's disturbing.

The great Australian leg-spinner Arthur Mailey always carried powdered resin in his pocket and when the umpire wasn't looking, he lifted the seam for the two fast bowlers.

One day, JWHT, the opposition captain, asked Mailey to show him his hand. He examined the hand carefully and said: 'Arthur, you've been using resin. I'll report you to the umpire.'

Mailey then asked JWHT to show him his right hand. He looked at the thumbnail and found it worn to the flesh on the outside.

'You've been lifting the seam, Johnny', Mailey said.

JWHT grinned and the matter was dropped.

All this happened 97 years before sandpaper made an entry into cricket's lexicon.

Johnny Douglas led England against Australia in two Test series.

64 HARRY TROTT

8 August 1898.

The Australian captain, while visiting his mother, collapsed and lost consciousness. Over the next few weeks, he was examined repeatedly but nothing conclusive could be found.

He continued to suffer from insomnia and memory loss.

Exactly nine months after he collapsed for the first time, he was admitted to a psychiatric hospital.

According to ace cricket writer Gideon Haigh, he was suffering from something similar to depressive psychosis, although it was not properly diagnosed.

He took years to recover but when he played cricket again, he scored 98 in 40 minutes. That signalled that he was indeed out of his troubles, albeit temporarily.

Armstrong, Chappelli, Border, Taylor, etc. are listed among the shrewd Australian captains but Harry Trott has been criminally forgotten.

The 1890s belonged to him.

He was a postman. When some other public servants complained about the frequent absence of Trott, the postal chief replied: 'Harry Trott is a national institution.'

His sense of humour made him acceptable to everyone in the team. Among Australian captains, only Lindsay Hassett could match him in that.

Going to bat in a game at Lord's, he put a lighted cigar aside.

He was out on the first ball. He returned calmly to the cigar, saying: 'Glad it hasn't gone out.'

Frank Iredale was having a tough time during one of the tours. One morning, Trott apparently told this teetotaller:

'Look here, Noss, what you need is a tonic. I'll mix you one.'

The drink worked well—Iredale scored a century in the Manchester Test.

Trott then revealed it was brandy and soda.

Once, driving against Johnny Briggs, Trott was out stumped but the umpire didn't see it properly. He repeated the shot next ball and walked to the pavilion. When he was accused of throwing his wicket away, he calmly replied: 'Little Briggsy had bowled himself inside out trying to trap me. Why should he be robbed because the umpire was out late last night?'

When Trott was returning from England in 1896, a reporter in Philadelphia asked him if he had ever heard of baseball.

Trott: 'Of course we have.'

Reporter: 'Then why don't you play it?'

Trott: 'Running around in circles makes us giddy…'

Harry Trott's name should be more well-known in cricketing circles. He deserves to considered among the great Australian cricket captains.

65 JACK D'ARCY

When 'The Invincibles' toured England in 1948, there were two cricketers who received all the letters from the fans.

One was Bradman. For being Bradman.

The other was Miller. For being the most charismatic among them all. Of course, all the ladies wrote to Miller.

Exactly ten years later, another cricketer became the heartthrob of young British women—a 22-year-old New Zealand batsman named Jack D'Arcy.

A handsome, smiling face, a mop of blondish hair, slight in stature—D'Arcy received hundreds of letters for every match he played in that tour.

He was known as 'The good-looking Jack'.

Years later, his daughter discovered stacks of mail among a pile of her father's cricket memorabilia, mainly from young women, expressing admiration for the touring 'pin-up' boy.

Result: an embarrassed father.

D'Arcy made his Test debut in that series and went on to play in all five Tests.

He never played another Test.

John Reid said of him: 'His courage and patience could never be questioned but his limited stroke equipment restricted his batting.'

He knew that he was not good enough to become a good cricketer.

He left the game at 25.

He spent 12 years with IBM in Sydney and a year in Singapore.

He had his own company in Sydney until he sold his business in 2000 to another company, which is now owned by Telstra.

Apart from being very successful in his professional career, D'Arcy tasted some success in the horse-racing circuit.

At one point, he owned 35 horses!

But, despite all this, his passion for his first love never faded.

He organised the 50-year reunion for the surviving members of the 1958 New Zealand team to England and nothing gives him more pleasure than playing the game and interacting with people learning the game.

He can still be found in Sydney, giving tips to a young boy with a bat in his hand.

Jack D'Arcy played cricket for a few years and then went on to have a successful corporate career.

66 CHUCK 'FLEETWOOD' SMITH

In 1990, constable Brian Graham was managing a one-man police station in a remote location just outside Victoria.

He had recently suffered a stroke and his wife was worried about his health.

She knew that one thing would help him for sure.

She had to make him talk about Chuck Fleetwood-Smith, in any way possible.

Quite miraculously, the chance came.

Graham got an opportunity to tell everything to Greg Growden, a young NSW-based journalist who was trying to write a book on Chuck.

Chuck was Graham's boyhood hero. In fact, Chuck was a hero to everyone in Stawell.

When Graham joined the police force in the 1960s, one of his initial tasks was to patrol the area around Flinders Station.

Graham came to know that his boyhood hero was living as a tramp under the bridge near the station.

He met him once and asked him about his cricket.

Chuck replied: 'That's over. All I want now is a meal, sleep, and a few beers.'

A few weeks later, one Mrs Enid Mason complained that Chuck and his mate had stolen her handbag.

A teary-eyed Graham had to arrest Chuck.

When Chuck appeared on the steps of the courthouse, Graham apologised to one of his family members: 'Your family must think I'm a bit of a bastard for arresting him. I'm very embarrassed. I really wish I had not done it. The other policemen have given me a hammering over this.'

Chuck's relative replied: 'No, no, no, you've got it all wrong. At least now we can do something about him, now we can save him. You've helped us save him.'

Chuck didn't drink after that episode. But the damage was already done, and he died a couple of years later.

Even 20 years after his death, constable Graham couldn't quite get over that episode and had tears in his eyes while recounting it to Growden.

But Chuck could bowl. On a good day, he was unplayable. On a bad day, he bowled like 'a hippie who gave away $25 million'.

And there was no one who could compete with his charisma.
Absolutely no one.

A teammate found him late one night in the team's hotel, leaning against the urinal, swaying slightly and appearing close to exhaustion. Asked what he was doing there, he quietly replied, 'Just having a rest before the next one.'
On some nights when Australia was on tour, he found no difficulty in 'slotting four or five women into his nightly schedule'.

During the 1960s, on an occasion, Bill O'Reilly found him proudly wearing his Test cap and drinking with a bunch of hobos.
Tiger grabbed him, shook him, and yelled: 'Abuse yourself, but don't abuse the cap.'
A chastened Chuck immediately took the baggy green

off and hid it down the front of his pants.

A wayward genius.
A genius nonetheless.

Chuck Fleetwood-Smith was a talented spinner who did well for Australia. In later life, he faced hardship and died in relative obscurity.

67 ROCKLEY WILSON

'It is right and reasonable that women should be able to vote in Parliamentary elections. There is no evidence to suppose that they are intellectually inferior to men', argued the young student in a discussion in the school's debating society. His motion was defeated by 36 votes to 12.

But Rockley Wilson was indomitable. He won the mile competition three years on the trot, scored runs for the first XI, excelled in rugby and racket games.

While doing all this, he spoke his mind and got reprimanded, all too often.

He was so talented that people used to enter his name in every possible competition. Once, Rockley was entered for a Latin competition without his knowledge. In a fit of panic, he obtained a copy of the previous entry and submitted it.

He was surprised at winning the prize but while accepting it, he confessed everything.

Many of the masters respected his honesty but he was still asked to leave.

He went to Trinity College, Cambridge and did well in all sports.

In 1903, he was invited to play a full season of county cricket prior to his taking up a teaching position at Winchester College.

All of a sudden, the cricket master at Winchester fell ill and Rockley was asked to start immediately. He threw himself into it, teaching cricket and French. In the classroom, his lessons were allegedly 30 per cent French and 70 per cent cricket.

Rockley had a rather rough and humiliating Great War.
He returned to Winchester in the summer of 1919.
Among the pupils waiting for him there was one

Douglas Jardine.

Rockley could penetrate the rather harsh exterior of Jardine and when, in 1932, he was informed that his most famous pupil was to lead England in Australia, he said: 'We shall win the Ashes— but we may lose a Dominion.'

Rockley Wilson had a huge library of cricket books and memorabilia.

One of the genuine well-wishers of the game of cricket.

There have been many better cricketers but Rockley Wilson was 'one of a kind' in his own way.

We seldom celebrate these people.

Rockley Wilson played his cricket for Cambridge University and Yorkshire. Also for England, in one Test match. He later became a popular coach.

68 DAVID SHEPPARD

According to one of his regular teammates at Sussex, 'If I could have been anybody in life, I'd have liked to have been David Sheppard.'

Jim Parks: 'David was the finest captain I ever played under.'

Alas.

He led Sussex only one summer. They challenged the 'invincible' Surrey for the title. He had led England in only two Test matches.

On 9 June 1953, at Grace Road, Leicester, he did prove his worth.

Leicester led by 345 after a couple of hours into the final day. The new ball was due. Sheppard took the new ball, handed it over to his fast bowler Jim Wood, and said: 'Don't take the ball out of its wrapping'. Wood looked perplexed.

Leicester had no money that season. The payment their players received that season was less than what the dustbin-men got. And the balls were a major item of expenditure.

Leicester already led by a handsome margin—no side had chased that many in the previous five years of county cricket.

Sheppard reiterated: 'Don't unwrap it, Woody. And, whatever you do, don't drop it'. He slowly started to change the field. It took forever.

Charles Palmer, the Leicestershire captain, came running down the stairs. He waved the batsmen in.

Sheppard took the ball from Wood's hand, chuckled, and murmured: 'I knew they couldn't afford a new ball'.

Less than four hours were left in the match. Sheppard opened the batting, scored an unbeaten 186, and took his team to victory with time to spare.

David Sheppard played 22 Test matches for England before becoming the Bishop of Liverpool.

69 FAROKH ENGINEER

'Engelbert Humperdinck—but only with his mouth shut!'

'Gay Cavalier'

'Pied Piper of Cricket'

John Arlott wrote: 'His cricket is spontaneous; he plays it as he does because it is his nature to enjoy the game, and he sees no reason to conceal that enjoyment.'

Well, Farokh Engineer did enjoy his game. He enjoys delivering after-dinner talks, mostly consisting of outrageous and apocryphal stories.

British cricket writer Douglas Miller once told me about his experiences with Farokh.

Late in 2009, he was researching his book on the ex-Lancashire captain Jack Bond (now in a sorry state, I have heard). Farokh was a huge fan of Bond.

'He had told me he was going abroad but would be back on a given date in December. He was very keen to talk as he loved Jack and rated him a terrific captain. I duly rang and felt that Farokh didn't sound quite his previous sparkling self. It turned out he was still in India and I had woken him in the middle of the night!'

Then, when the book was published without Farokh's inputs, Miller went to his home in Lancashire to present him a copy.

Farokh was watching television—highlights of golf which he thought was live!

Miller already knew the name of the winner. He broke the news to Farokh.

Farokh chuckled, finished eating a lovely curry, got up, and went out to play bridge.

Farokh Engineer played Test cricket for India.

70 ARTHUR MAILEY

There are greats and then there are favourites.

In the second list, among Australians, if I have to pick six, they would be Arthur Mailey, Lindsay Hassett, Bill Johnston, Sid Barnes, Alan Davidson, and Wally Grout.

After a visit to the Art Gallery of New South Wales, Mailey encountered an anonymous benefactor who showed him Bernard Bosanquet's wrong 'un.

Armed with the new weapon, he rushed home like 'somebody who had found a nugget of gold'. It indeed was.

He had passed it on to Clarrie Grimmett and then to Bill O'Reilly, then to Richie Benaud… and we know where it ended.

When Australia's nationalistic team manager reprimanded Mailey for showing his tricks to English leg-spinner Ian Peebles, Mailey replied: 'Please understand that slow bowling is an art. And art is international.'

Thank goodness we had people like Mailey playing cricket. And then writing one of the best autobiographies by a Test cricketer.

Cartoonist, writer, cricketer, humourist. Arthur Mailey was good enough to fit in all these roles.

71 LINDSAY HASSETT

His brother, due to get married, waited for him, on 92, to get the century. Exasperated after a while, he left to get married, with him batting on 96.

Came back to see him on 97!

He later said: 'I got my century before he went on his honeymoon.'

Lindsay Hassett was pretty special. None in that famous Australian team was as witty and humorous as him.

Surely he was the only captain in international cricket history to eat his meal in a five-star hotel in his shirt, tie, and underpants.

At an official function early in the 1953 tour, he began his speech with: 'Never in my life have I seen so many ugly men or (after a brief pause) so many beautiful women. If it were the other way round, I would not be here.'

He had bowled the second last over of the Oval Test and at the end of the match said: 'England deserved to win, if not from the first ball, at least from the second-last over.'

When he was later congratulated for his speech, he quickly replied: 'Thank you. It wasn't bad, considering that Tony Lock chucked half the side out.'

There are many good cricketers today but not many characters like Lindsay Hassett.

Jack McHarg's book on him has the subtitle *One of a Kind*, which he surely was.

He has always been a favourite of mine.

Lindsay Hassett succeeded Bradman as the captain of Australia. The wittiest among them all.

72 LIONEL TENNYSON

May 1987.

Hampshire captain Mark Nicholas brought his mother into the pristine county club.

Upon entering, they turned right and began to climb the stairs when, at the first level, she stopped.

She was staring at a photograph.

'Lionel, Lionel Tennyson… Lionel played for Hampshire?'

Nicholas looked embarrassed.

'Either side of the first war, Lionel Tennyson *was* Hampshire. Surely you knew that. He captained the county for… er… well, for years.'

Long before Colin Ingleby-Mackenzie's 'wine, women, and song' slogan, it was Lionel Tennyson who instilled that culture in the Hampshire team.

When Hampshire played in London, he went straight from the cricket to *White's Club*, of which he had been a member for many years.

There he would dine well, play cards till morning, take a Turkish bath, and return to the ground for the day's play.

And his rule on the field of play was absolute. No one ever had the temerity to oppose him.

On an occasion, one of the batsmen was felled by a bouncer. As he sat on the ground, a note was brought to him.

'What do you think your _____ bat is for? signed Lionel'

On another occasion, he tried to intimidate the umpire.

As a batsman came out to join him at the crease towards the end of the day, Tennyson, seeing the poor light, shouted out, 'Are you there?'

The incoming batsman replied, 'I can hear you, my Lord,

but I can't see you.'

He could have given the likes of Bill Edrich and Keith Miller a run for their money.

Both on the field and off it!

He was injured thrice in World War I and from that point, decided to live each day as it was the last in his life.

How else could one justify selling off a new Rolls Royce to pay for a bad evening at the card table?

And long before Malcolm Marshall, he batted one-handed in a Test match, that too against the likes of McDonald and Gregory.

Lionel Tennyson was one of the true characters of the game. A Hampshire legend.

Behind the Scenes

73 KEN MEDLOCK

'You must be out of your tiny minds. You're liquidating the best-known name in the game of cricket!', shouted the newly elected board member of the Non-Food Sub Committee.

It was the first meeting he was attending at the Co-Operative Wholesale Society headquarters in Manchester.

For 16 years, the Co-op had owned John Wisden & Co.

There had been a recommendation to liquidate it.

No one else around him had any idea about the might of the name.

He continued: 'I don't know why it's losing money. I want to know much more about this.'

The proposal was withdrawn and he was made the chairman.

Ken Medlock was born in 1914. In 1921, he first watched cricket. He saw Charles Macartney score a classy century.

He started his journey as a ball boy for the Birch Vale Cricket Club in Derbyshire and Cheshire League.

In a decade or so, he graduated to the first team.

They were led by Joe Milburn, who often brought his little boy Colin with him.

As soon as he began the daunting task of reviving John Wisden & Co., he discovered that they were selling all possible cricket products via departmental stores!

The average age of the ball-makers startled him: 73!

He set up a joint ball-making venture with Surridges, Gray-Nicholls, and Ives.

He had two choices for promoting the bats: Geoff Boycott and John Hampshire.

On the basis of temperament, Hampshire was chosen—no surprises there.

In 1963, he, along with West Indian great Learie Constantine, convinced the MCC and the WICB to agree to their proposal of presenting the Wisden Trophy to the winner of the West Indies v England series.

By the end of the 1960s, *Wisden* was economically sound.

In the old factory outlet, some old bats were waiting to be burnt when Medlock visited the place.

Those bats belonged to the likes of Grace, Ranji, Trumper, and Jessop.

In those days, cricket memorabilia wasn't a popular interest.

'Right, you can have them', he was told.

A decade after saving *Wisden*, he saved those bats as well.

Some of those bats have found a place in Lord's, a few others in Old Trafford.

In 2006, aged 91, he flew to Australia to donate the Trumper bat to the Bradman Museum.

The airport people thought it was a weapon and the bat ended up in the captain's cabin before being handed over to the Museum.

Ken Medlock, aged 105 at the time of writing, has lost a lot of his memory.

His sons are negotiating the sale of his collection of bats to Lord's.

But he still remembers his beloved Old Trafford.

And, perhaps, Macartney's batting on that hot day in 1921.

Ken Medlcok was the Chairman of John Wisden & Co in the 1960s. A life-long cricket lover who, in various capacities, has contributed to the preservation of the rich history of the game.

74 IRVING ROSENWATER

Early 2000s.

A cricket auction in London.

A 70-year-old man wandering down the corridors, crying out at the top of his voice that some of his limited edition pamphlets had just fetched world-record prices for a living cricket author.

This man possessed the most amazing collection of books.

When asked what would happen to his collection after his death, he snorted: 'I shall burn it.'

Thank goodness that didn't happen.

It weighed four tonnes. The bookseller Christopher Saunders was entrusted by the collector's sister to sell it.

In 1949, a letter was sent to the editor of *The Cricketer*. It was written by a 17-year-old named Irving Rosenwater.

'Allow me to correct an error which appears in the current issue of your fine paper...'

A year later, there was another letter:

'May I be permitted to point out one or two omissions which have occurred in the recent publication of minor counties records...'

His first article was published in 1956—*The Hazards of Cricket*, describing injuries suffered by cricketers, cricket people, and even spectators.

In 1960, he was commissioned to write a regular feature: *Feats, Facts, and Figures*.

A few years later, he joined Rowland Bowen's camp and contributed to his scholarly journal *The Cricket Quarterly*.

The friendship between two of the most eccentric cricket people lasted only a few months.

Years later, Rosenwater wrote in a letter to Murray Hedgcock: 'I have written 10,000 words on Bowen which have lain idle—deliberately idle—for it would be damaging for any writer to publish an appraisal of that man.'

Rosenwater was the finest statistician and historian (rare to have both qualities in one man) of his day. He worked for the BBC till he opted to work for Kerry Packer's World Series Cricket.

He flew with teams from city to city till he was banned by the airline for a rather shameful incident involving an air-hostess.

In the 1980s, he stopped making frequent public appearances and decided to only reply to correspondences sent to him by first-class mail.

In 1968, Rosenwater became the first historian to unearth the second innings batting order of all English and Australian teams that played against each other.

Ten years later, he wrote the definitive book on Don Bradman.

The man is largely forgotten, and he deserves a biography.

But who'll play with fire?

Irving Rosenwater was a leading authority on the history and statistics of the game in the post-war years.

75 SIEGFRIED SASSOON

He usually positioned himself at mid-on.

When the batsman hit the ball towards him, he could often not find enough time to move.

The ball usually cracked against his unprotected shins.

He would be in pain, but would pick up the ball and gently throw it underarm to the bowler.

And he was perhaps the worst catcher of the cricket ball.

According to his close friend Edmund Blunden, at his peak, he had a batting average of just under 17.

Blunden exaggerated—it was much lower than that.

But Siegfried Sassoon never shied away from playing the game of cricket. In fact, he needed to play it on most days.

His father left him when he was four.

He modelled himself on his artist mother and became a poet.

He did well in the first year of the Great War. But gradually, he became disillusioned with the War and sent a letter of defiance to his commanding officer.

He was to be court-martialled.

The poet Robert Graves saved him, but he was sent to the hospital for treatment, where he met Wilfred Owen.

They were together for two and half months.

Sassoon had a great influence on Owen and yet, when Owen died a year later, Sassoon was the first to admit that Owen was the greater war-poet.

The only friendship in his lonely life lasted just 80-odd days.

Sassoon the war poet died in 1919. After a few homosexual encounters, he declared that he was gay, a remarkable thing to do in the 1920s.

He lived till 1967—lonely, unfulfilled, yet rhapsodic.

Cricket writer David Foot summed it up well:

'Sassoon needed his loneliness. The loneliness he cherished most of all was in the crowded, silent company of the timeless trees; in the company of the nuns and the monks who could communicate without conversation; and, maybe above all, amid the sublime innocence of a freshly mown outfield.'

Siegfried Sassoon was a leading poet, writer, and soldier. And a life-long cricket enthusiast.

76 DICK BRITTENDEN

'I worship Cardus', he once said.

But then, a few years later, he understood the flaws in Cardus' work.

He changed his style of writing and wrote: 'I believe that in sports reporting, it is essential to be honest and not betray any confidences. If you do, you've got a story, but you've lost a news source and perhaps a friend.'

I do not know of any other cricket writer who underwent this kind of change in his style midway through his career.

Dick Brittenden had a rough war. Like many others, once the war ended, cricket made life easier for him.

In 1955, he was instrumental in setting up a sports department at The Christchurch Press, He remained the editor there till the mid-1980s.

People bought the newspaper to read his articles.

The turning point in his career was the Johannesburg Test match in 1953, famous for Sutcliffe's and Blair's heroics.

He wrote: 'We were all white as sheets and the top South African writer Louis Duffus had tears running down his cheeks.'

Silver Fern on the Veldt happened and Brittenden became a well-known name in cricketing circles.

Another 14 books followed.

New Zealand sportswriter Lynn McConnell says: 'Some of his books are the only real connection many people have with the past of the game here.'

Brittenden, along with Don Cameron, inspired a generation of New Zealand cricket writers who went on to produce some underrated gems.

A nice man who is largely forgotten. If he was alive, he

would have chuckled at that before going out for a round of golf.

And there too, as ace cricket historian David Frith once found out in Wellington, 'he would be very understanding of the faulty play and irritating stoppages for lost balls'.

Dick Brittenden is perhaps the most famous cricket writer from New Zealand. He wrote extensively on cricket and inspired many in that country to take up cricket journalism/writing.

77 JOHN WOODCOCK

The 14-year-old was a natural ball player who was good at most games.

But then tragedy struck.

One fine day, he found difficulty in walking and had to visit the doctor.

Septic arthritis in the hip, and it had poisoned badly.

No antibiotics.

Four months of hanging from a frame to prevent it from spreading.

Six hip replacements later, he still lived for the love of his life.

John Woodcock is ancient. His grandfather was born before the Battle of Waterloo.

He was EW Swanton's cameraman and assistant during the 1950–51 Ashes. Three years later, he was elevated to the post of the cricket correspondent of *The Times*.

He had sat on CB Fry's knees. He had played golf with Herbert Sutcliffe and Len Hutton.

He had gone duck-shooting with Harold Larwood.

He had taken a stumping off Bill O'Reilly and had batted with Wally Hammond.

He still remembers Colin Cowdrey's first Test century and claims that he has not seen a better hundred in 82 years of watching cricket.

When Cowdrey was sent for in 1974-75, almost 20 years after his maiden hundred, to take on Dennis Lillee and Jeff Thomson at the WACA, Perth, Woodcock said he felt as shaky as if his own son were walking out to bat. He had to take himself off to the bar to calm his nerves.

There were a lot of complaints about Basil D'Oliveira's night life in the West Indies in 1968. The editor of *The*

Sunday Times rung Woodcock to discuss about writing a rather spicy piece on that topic. Woodcock told him he wasn't interested in that kind of journalism.

He has never written a book or an autobiography because, as he says: 'I know too much about what really went on.'

Surely he would have found the current match reports intolerable, the ones with headlines like *5 things India must do to beat England.*

Cricket's friend. Cricketers' friend.
John Woodcock has been one of a kind.

John Woodcock has watched more than 400 Test matches and has covered the game for over 60 years.

78 PETER WYNNE-THOMAS

'One day the door opened and an elderly man who introduced himself as a relative of Shrewsbury came in. I asked him, "Have you got any old letters in the attic?"

'He said: "Yes!"'

Peter Wynne-Thomas had been waiting for two years. He did everything to find someone who could help him with information about Arthur Shrewsbury's family.

Wynne-Thomas capitalised on the letters by determinedly digging out all the other surviving relatives, enabling the construction of the definitive Shrewsbury family tree in his book *Give Me Arthur*.

He had always been intensely dedicated to cricket history, following rigorous and scholarly standards.

In 1970, he was all set to take over the editorship of *Cricket Quarterly* from Rowland Bowen.

But then, Bowen wrote his book on cricket history and suddenly thought that the journal was too personal a project to be given to someone else.

In his free time, Wynne-Thomas conducted a Haygarth-esque survey to find more about old Nottinghamshire cricketers. He made a book out of the material and it won the Cricket Society award in 1971.

In 1973, he, along with Robert Brooke, found the Association of Cricket Statisticians. The impact of ACS on cricket research all over the world is huge. Wynne-Thomas deserves a lot of credit for that.

He has been a cricket researcher for over fifty years and is one of the very few who have been able to support themselves and their family by doing nothing else.

Eric Midwinter once told me a bit about Wynne-

Thomas:

'I was at Trent Bridge watching England getting battered by the West Indies (1995). I saw all of a gloriously classic attacking century by Brian Lara. The I went in search of Peter. There he was, tucked away in his library, preparing an index of the *Cricketer* magazine with never a thought for the cricket happening a few yards away.'

Arthur Haygarth was the leading cricket historian in the 19th century. Peter Wynne-Thomas has been the librarian and historian at Trent Bridge for many decades.

79 R.C. ROBERTSON-GLASGOW

Somerset v Gloucestershire in 1953.

A 24-year-old journalist finally met the great cricket writer. It was the only time he had met him.

'He had sat silently behind most of us for the whole of the day's play, eventually scribbling his piece for *The Observer*, I believe. In a quiet, courteous voice, he asked if he could borrow my phone to send his match report to London. Only when he began his dictation did I realise who he was. Nothing in my life was more willingly donated.'

On 4 March 1965, the snow was falling heavily. Elizabeth went out with a shovel to clear a path to the gate. It was hard work and took some time. When she returned to the house, her husband was unconscious. He had taken a massive overdose. The inquest concluded that a morbid fear of snow contributed to the cause of death.

Not everyone agreed to that. People who knew him well were not convinced with the explanation.

It was in the genes. His father had not been the most mature of men. His brother suffered from bouts of anxiety.

The novelist Graham Greene, a distant cousin, suffered from depression.

Moreover, he had a forgettable childhood. His father was not mentally fit to take care of him. His mother was often too stern with her children.

The young man embraced the game of cricket. He found peace when he played it.

But, when things were not going well, the 'Black Dog' crept up on him.

But Raymond Robertson-Glasgow could write. He could write well. He could, in fact, write very well. He wrote as much as possible—often to avoid the demons.

He once wrote a paragraph on a pre-war Somerset batsman who steadfastly refused cucumber with his salad lunch. The player claimed that it gave him red spots in front of his eyes.

'And left him with a tricky decision, back at the crease, not knowing for certain which was the correct ball.'

That 24-year-old journalist, named David Foot, later wrote: 'Pure Wodehouse. Or should it be pure Robertson-Glasgow?'

'…been my literary hero and my unattainable model…'

Raymond Robertson-Glasgow is regarded as one of the finest cricket writers. He is famous for his short essays on contemporary cricketers.

80 TONY COZIER

In 1966, there were repeated letters to the BBC complaining about the employment of a 'black bastard'.

That 'black bastard' was accustomed to seeing jaws drop when people met him for the first time and discovered that he was not black.

The 25-year-old was the visiting commentator on Test Match Special.

This was his second trip to England.

In 1963, he covered the Test series as a freelancer, often sleeping in YMCAs and friends' sofas.

For the next 50 years, he was pretty much the voice of West Indian cricket.

He possessed a wonderful zest for life. He loved to party and threw bashes close to his beach hut on the east coast of Barbados.

Everybody was invited, and most journalists found a way to reach there.

Vic Marks met him in Cardiff in 2013 and described how full of life he was even at that age.

'Towards the end of a meal in the basement of an Italian restaurant there came the strains of Elvis Presley. Tony's antennae were alerted: he started to sing. The diners at the next table were South Africans following the cricket, and, it turned out, just as keen on Elvis. And there was Tony, delicately dancing around the tables with one of the wives, a smile on his face, and a sparkle in his eye.'

In an age when commentators compare W.G. Grace's batting with that of Sunil Narine, Tony Cozier is sorely missed.

Tony Cozier is widely regarded as the voice of West Indies cricket.

81 JIM KILBURN

When Maurice Leyland bowled to Bradman, he wrote: 'No one expected him to get a wicket, he was neither good enough nor bad enough for that.'

But those were serious match reports. Jim Kilburn was serious and dedicated.

As a young boy, he was tutored by the great George Hirst in the Scarborough nets. His off-breaks were good enough to make him an important player in the Bradford League.

During the off-season, he taught at Harrogate Prep School. He then got a chance to spend a year in Finland, from where he used to send travel articles to the *Yorkshire Post*.

They were pretty good. On his return, the editor Arthur Mann wanted to meet him. Kilburn managed to impress him.

Mann was startled by his interest in the game of cricket.

AW Pullin had retired three years ago, and *The Post* had no cricket correspondent at that time.

Kilburn was put on probation for three months at a weekly wage of £3.

His first assignment was a Roses Match at Sheffield. He did a good job. Neville Cardus wrote to the newspaper and said of Kilburn: 'To my mind, yours is the best cricket reporting today.'

That was good enough for him to secure a permanent position.

Kilburn was one of those few who got a regular by-line. No one was allowed to touch his writing, nor did any editor ever make any changes to his words.

He had his own methods, which worked well for him. Here's what David Frith recollects about the man: 'During the classic Oval Test match of 1968, it was my duty to deliver his story to the office of the *Yorkshire Post* in Fleet Street as soon as he had completed it. Today's cricket writers would laugh at the ponderous process.'

JMK was probably the last journalist to write his copy with a fountain pen, creating the same sort of broad sweeps of script as his Victorian predecessors. The sheets of paper were then carefully folded and placed in an envelope, which young Frith received with barely a glance from the writer. It was now a challenge for the bus or tube journey, followed by a spring down Fleet Street, culminating in a breathless hurtling up the stairs into the newspaper office.

Kilburn always watched every ball in a day's play except for the first half hour in the post-lunch session. That time was allotted for his afternoon nap. His great friend Bill Bowes covered for him.

'As I look around me now in the so-called "media centres," with the predominantly history-allergic writers and their mass of electronic gadgetry, I do sometimes picture the reassuring picture of JMK with his solemn, shrewd gaze, his imposing nose…, and, of course, that thick-nib pen which he used to put to such charming use,' Frith recalls.

It was said that Cardus was the Wordsworth and Kilburn the Coleridge of immediate post-war cricket writing.
Kilburn wrote fewer lies and, perhaps, as a result, attracted less public attention.
Once in Adelaide, he finished his account with 'At the kerbside, five or six strikingly attractive young ladies were standing beneath a sign that read: Queue for Kilburn. An envious companion assured me that the girls were merely waiting for a local bus.'

Jim Kilburn was a leading cricket writer from Yorkshire.

82 RAY ROBINSON

Bill O'Reilly: 'Of all the cricket writers I have read and tried to read, Ray Robinson was the unrivalled leader of the band.'

Alan Davidson: 'His books were masterpieces, the research was incredible. He was not just a writer; he was a friend of cricket.'

During World War II, as the sub-editor for *Daily Telegraph*, Robinson started writing a book.

He called it *Between Wickets*.

By then, he was a friend of Neville Cardus and didn't hesitate to send the manuscript to him.

Cardus was so impressed after reading it that he sent it on to William Collins, the renowned publisher.

The book was published in 1946 and was reprinted five times in four years. Collins was happy and more books followed.

Robinson's classic work on Australia's cricket captains *On Top Down Under* won The Cricket Society Literary Award in 1976.

But it was *Between Wickets* that made him famous and well-known all over the cricketing world. He once said: 'You know, *Between Wickets* was good to me. It enabled me to buy our house at Northbridge.'

While reviewing the book, RC Robertson-Glasgow wrote, 'A book to be read; every line of it; and not to be lent without an I.O.U.'

Indeed. If you care for cricket's history, please read this book. Not many better cricket books have been written over all these years.

P.S. Now there is a cricket journal named *Between Wickets*. Not surprisingly, over the last few years, it has become the best cricket journal/magazine in the world.

Ray Robinson was the first great Australian cricket writer.

83 ROGER PAGE

'I have combed the internet, but in vain. One or two sellers in the U.K. have it but they are not very keen to ship the magazines to India. Perhaps you can help?'

'Okay. I will arrange all 24 issues by the end of the year.'

This was in June 2017. For a couple of years, I had been desperate to get hold of a complete run of *Wisden Cricket Monthly*. No one could assure me like that.

'Do you have the two volumes of *Webster*? And *Post-Padwick* by Gibbs?'

'I do have the two volumes. I will get a copy of *Post-Padwick* in a few months.'

When I met Gideon Haigh, he told me that there are two places in the world that I must visit.

David Frith's house in Guildford, Surrey, and Roger Page's house in Yallambie, Victoria.

When he was 12 years old, he came to Australia. When he was 21, he wrote a book on the history of Tasmanian cricket.

Then, in June 1969, he went to England to acquire stock.

In October 1969, he published his first catalogue.

It's been 49 years.

Roger Page has never failed to publish a catalogue on a bi-monthly basis since 1973.

When I asked him about his early days, he was honest:

'I got into dealing, at first from Tasmania, as a means of increasing the personal library and making contact with other collectors in Australia.

'The first customers were mainly subscribers to the serious English cricket periodical *The Cricket Quarterly* (I was appointed as the Australian agent in 1965).

'It was a part-time business for three years, with the taxman taking all the profits!

'I moved to Melbourne in late 1971 and set up the business full-time, working from home. Took about four years to become fully established.'

He could continue only because his wife provided financial support during those early years.

He never says 'no' because he is always confident that he'll be able to find 'that book'.

And nothing stops him from finding those rare books—despite multiple surgeries in the last 12 months, he has made a successful 'comeback' every time.

Australia's last specialist cricket bookseller is 83 years young at the time of writing.

Roger Page has been a cricket book dealer/ seller for 50 years.

84 MATTHEW ENGEL

At the *Wisden* dinner at the East India Club in April 1992, Graeme Wright stepped down from the post of editor of the *Wisden Cricketers' Almanack*.

In his words, he was not enjoying anymore and said that cricket had become too much of a business and cultural rot had set in.

The search for a new editor settled on an existing contributor, Matthew Engel.

He had, by then, experience of 20 years and had already co-edited three editions of a reference work—*The Sportspages Almanac*.

He was on the verge of finishing a history of the Northamptonshire CCC for the Christopher Helm series.

The most he expected was Wright asking him to do the book reviews. Instead, Wright asked him to do the whole thing.

Newspapers didn't welcome this choice and termed Engel an 'iconoclast'.

He started to work and immediately began to make changes he thought were necessary.

The *Almanack* was re-arranged into six parts: Comments, Records, English cricket, Overseas cricket, Administration and Laws, and Miscellaneous.

He introduced an orthodox contents page. He pushed the index to the back.

He also introduced the immensely valuable and popular *Cricket Round the World*.

He dropped the *List of Oxbridge Blues*.

In 1996, he started the World Championship of Test cricket by simply awarding points for wins. In 2003, ICC adopted this idea and refined it to come up with the current set of rankings.

He made Sanath Jayasuriya a *Wisden* Cricketer of the Year, despite him not playing any part in the preceding English summer.

By the end of that decade, Engel had led *Wisden* through a thorough transformation.

In 2001, Engel flew west to become *The Guardian's* correspondent in Washington.

'It seems like time to let someone else have a crack', he said.

He also pointed out that even his famous predecessor Sydney Pardon 'did not have to report and explain defeats against New Zealand.'

He came back in 2004 and the very next year his son Laurie became seriously ill.

He covered the 2005 Ashes in great detail while sitting by the side of his ailing son at the Birmingham hospital.

His son died of cancer. Engel, though drowned in grief, somehow managed to produce the most successful of editions (2006).

His remarks were often hard-hitting.

In 2000, he wrote: 'The County Championship's prime trouble is not that it is unwatched but that it is unwatchable.'

He also stated that the ICC assemble the world's best players and get them to play bad cricket.

Engel always believed that 'cricket managed simultaneously to be absurdly trivial and desperately important.'

He himself is one of the most important figures in the history of the *Bible of Cricket*.

Matthew Engel has been a prominent figure at The Guardian *and* Wisden.

85 STEPHEN CHALKE

7 October 1997.

An unknown writer self-publishes his first book—on county cricket in the 1950s.

At a time when Simon Hughes' *A Lot of Hard Yakka* is getting all the attention in the U.K.

A few weeks later, Stephen Chalke, the author, gets a call from Frank Keating. Keating says it's the best he has read in a long, long time and will be writing the same in his column for *The Guardian*.

Another few weeks later, the author finds that E.W. Swanton has listed it among his six best cricket books of all time.

And then he finds John Major saying that it is one of the best books he has ever read.

Michael Parkinson's column on the book in *The Daily Telegraph* reaches the most number of readers and the 1,500 copies printed vanish in a few days.

Another 1,000 copies by spring 1998.
And another 800 by spring 1999.

3,300 copies. All gone. We are now left with the occasional and often overpriced copies on Amazon and AbeBooks.

Thankfully, Stephen Chalke continued to write.
More importantly, he continued to write high-quality stuff for a period of over 20 years.

And has published many quality books written by others.

A year or so ago, I decided to gather everything he has written so far.

All the books, the essays in *Wisden Cricket Monthly, The Times, The Independent, Wisden Cricketer,* and *The Almanack.*
And the two pieces for *The Journal of The Cricket Society.*

I have managed to find them all—even the first piece he ever wrote.
No, not on cricket. It was on chess, written in the 1970s.

I have not yet gone this far for anyone else.

As he always says: 'It was a labour of love. As cricket should always be.'

Recently retired, Stephen Chalke wrote on cricket over the last 22 years.

86 ALAN GIBSON

A mild schizophrenic.
A manic depressive.

'Almost every aspect of his character had its exact opposite somewhere else in his psyche. He could be perfectly charming—and an utter bastard.

'He was an intensely sociable man—much given to condemning people whom he hardly knew as "bloody fools" on the flimsiest of evidence.

'He could moralise about the sins of the flesh with all the fervour of a dissenting preacher—and then go out drinking and womanising.

'He could be generous to a fault—and vicious to a degree.

'He was highly self-motivated—yet his problems were someone else's fault.

'He was devoted to his wives and children—and frequently made their lives a misery.'

—A son on his father.

Alan Gibson was an infant prodigy. He made his debut as a journalist at the age of nine, as editor of his class magazine at Farmer Road Elementary School, Leyton.

He used to write long essays and when away from his parents, they became long letters.
He gained a First in history at Oxford without attending a single lecture.

He had the military police knocking on his door when he failed to turn up for a medical. He always argued that an evening with C.B. Fry was an obvious priority.

He often viewed play with his back to the field. In one hand was invariably a weighty book of classical substance, in the other a tumbler that was rarely empty.

He was possibly the only writer who could write a match report even if there was no play at all.

Apart from John Arlott, everyone else shivered at the prospect of sharing the commentary box with him. No, not because of what you think. But because they knew they had no way of matching his erudition and knowledge. His academic mien always shone out.

Unfortunately, the booze got the better of him in the end. John Woodcock made a desperate attempt to bring him back to 'life'.

He wanted Gibson to update H.S. Altham and E.W. Swanton's *History of Cricket*. Swanton was very keen, but Gibson's will to work had faded and desolation was setting in.

There were people who took *The Times* and *The Cricketer* to just read his pieces. And most of these people knew little or nothing about cricket.

That was what Alan Gibson was capable of.
If only…

Alan Gibson wrote delightful pieces on cricket, usually for The Times *and* The Cricketer.

87 GERARD BRODRIBB

'Just like Jessop, sonny, just like Jessop', shouted the old man seating beside the nine-year-old.

Maurice Tate had made a roof-wrecking blow and it had brought down a shower of slates around the kid.

All this happened in the Hastings ground.

Fifty years later, he wrote a book on Jessop. Another two years and his book on Tate was published.

A decade or so later, there was a book on cricket in Hastings.

Gerald Brodribb never forgot anything from his first visit to a county match. The result was these three books.

But Brodribb was famous even before all this.

In 1952, *Next Man In: A Survey of Cricket Laws and Customs* was published. It made him well-known in cricketing circles. But the humble researcher was not satisfied. Some of his letters to the editor of The Cricketer made it clear that he was there to find out more about the laws of the game.

Then, in 1997, he wrote a book on underarm bowling. He had gone through all possible books and journals to find references of lob bowling and listed down all that in the book.

'His work in cricket was painstaking, but alas almost unrecognised now, in this frantic age', is what David Frith has to say about Brodribb.

Then there's this report in *The Times*, dated 23 September 2007:

'A Roman bath house with remains of plunge pools, steam rooms and clothes lockers is for sale in the town of

Battle, East Sussex. Built for officers of the Roman navy in about AD90, the baths are on the market for a modest £300,000.

'The baths were excavated in 1970 by Gerald Brodribb, an amateur archaeologist who identified the remains with divining rods and set about digging with a team of 40 enthusiasts.'

Brodribb found remnants of two steam rooms, three plunge pools, and two changing rooms with lockers.

All this resulted in a book on *Roman Brick and Tile* in 1987. He was a brilliant researcher irrespective of the subject in question.

A charming man by all accounts.

He wrote a book on six-hitting. In the mid-1990s, a Somerset supporter named Barry Phillips read about Arthur Wellard's exploits in that book. He contacted Brodribb, who was kind enough to share the interviews he took of Wellard.

All the material from Brodribb got Phillips going and resulted in a very readable biography of Wellard.

Gerald Brodribb is a forgotten man.

The sad part is that even the serious aficionados of the game no longer value his contribution.

Gerald Brodribb was a cricket researcher. A real keen student of the great game.

88 SCYLD BERRY

The 13-year-old was away for a vacation with his father. He was glued to the radio, listening to cricket commentary.

England were playing against Pakistan at Lord's.

The two of them were having breakfast when his sister Melloney rang from home.

There was news. His mother had suffered a brain haemorrhage.

They hastily returned home. All through the way, he was still listening to the commentary on radio.

They reached the hospital and heard that there had been a severe second haemorrhage.

As Hanif Mohammad battled to save the match for Pakistan, his mother battled against death.

Hanif succeeded. His mother couldn't.

'I do not remember crying much, or feeling angry or bitter, or even talking. Cricket kept me going—firstly reading about it, then writing it, before I ever had a chance to play.'

Scyld Berry was six years old when he first went through the pages of a Wisden.

It fascinated him.

Seven years later, after his mother died, he immersed himself in the Yorkshire CCC yearbooks.

His father was a teacher who was too absent-minded to look after his children. The children, in fact, knew that they had to look after their father.

Rescued by Hanif and Yorkshire CCC yearbooks, Berry began to explore the game of cricket even more.

In the early 1970s, still an undergraduate in Cambridge, he submitted his first article to David Frith, the editor of *The Cricketer*.

It was published.

Five years later, *The Observer* sent him to cover an overseas tour with the England team.

Then, in the early 1980s, he wrote *CricketWallah*. In that book, he predicted that cricket in India would take off and it wouldn't be long before they would become the superpower in world cricket.

He followed it up with another book on cricket in the subcontinent in 1987 (Cricket Odyssey).

He has edited Wisden, apart from covering the highest number of overseas tours by an English journalist.

He not only wrote good books himself but also gave birth to ideas behind great cricket books.

He persuaded Stephen Chalke to write the book on Geoffrey Howard.

A decade later, he (along with Chalke) coaxed an autobiography out of David Foot.

Berry still plays the game. He bowls gentle leg-breaks for Hinton Charterhouse Cricket Club. And continues to idolise Shakespeare and Hammond.

It's cricket that has kept him going for so long.

For him, it's been *The Game of Life*.

Scyld Berry has been the leading cricket journalist in England over the last three decades.

89 DAVID FOOT

He was barely eight years old when he had sent his superficial psychological tale to the then-famous *Strand Magazine*.

The magazine's regular contributors included the likes of PG Wodehouse, Arthur Conan Doyle, GK Chesterton, Rudyard Kipling, HG Wells, and Max Beerbohm.

But this child had no idea about such names. His contribution had been written in a school exercise book in red ink.

He imagined the reply would be accompanied by a modest cheque. The reply arrived in four days but there was no cheque. Instead, there was editorial rebuke in a letter:

'Just don't waste our time with rubbish like this. And at least make some effort in presenting it properly.'

The magazine closed in 1950. Our subject, by then 21, shed no tears. He had already started his career as a journalist.

When the Bristol Evening World closed in 1961, big-time Fleet Street seriously wooed him. He preferred to be a freelancer.

He chose to stay in the part of England where he grew up and not to seek his fortune among the national papers in London. He doesn't regret that. The essence of his work is his provincialism, his roots in the west country.

'Cricket writing was always to me more about the man than his runs. I chased Tom Graveney across golf courses to try to discover the volume of his dissatisfaction for Tom Pugh, the Old Etonian who was being brought in to lead Gloucestershire at Tom's expense. Stamina too often came into the job. I spent days chasing round the country trying to locate that lovely Pakistan batsman, Zaheer Abbas, the subject of another of my ghosting exercises. Apart from any other considerations, I had no journalistic regrets at being held along with my wife at gunpoint in Lahore. Who rightly says that the most enthralling sport is away from the ground?'

The two book of essays (*Beyond Bat and Ball* and *Fragments of Idolatry*) and those two superb biographies (on Wally Hammond and Harold Gimblett) are good enough to place him among the best cricket writers.

David Foot has written on the game for over fifty years. He specialised on the West country from where he belonged.

90 RUSSELL CROWE

'I found this wood in trench at Canakkale the same day your Australians ran away. All day, I watched them use it on the beach. Through bomb and bullets. They never stopped. I kept it—to remind me of that victory day. You tell me. It is a game or weapon?', asked the Turkish soldier who was helping Connor locate bodies.

Connor smiled and replied: 'Both, in the right hands. Here, give it to me.'

Connor, an Australian, travelled to Turkey post the Gallipoli debacle to look for his lost or dead sons.

This is the storyline of the movie *The Water Diviner*—Russell Crowe's directorial debut. He himself played the role of Connor.

The film was set in the year 1915. Crowe, a bit of a perfectionist, wanted to make a replica of the bat used by Monty Noble during the 1905 Ashes series. After some serious research, Michael Fahey found that Noble had used an 'Ayres Bat' for that season in England. Crowe made sure an exact replica was made.

Neither the make of the bat nor the homage to Monty Noble was mentioned in the film. For Crowe, it didn't matter. He knew the bat was right and that was all that mattered.

Crowe is a cousin of the famous cricketing brothers Martin and Jeff. He has not played much cricket but is obsessed with the game.

In 2006, Martin wanted to sell his collection of cricket memorabilia. Martin knew how to value the rich history of the game and his collection was an impressive one.

As soon as Russell came to know of his plans, he bought it all from Martin.

Russell has his own museum in Nymboida and the

collection is on display there for the general public.

So, it didn't look like a publicity stunt when, five days after the Phil Hughes tragedy, he walked onto the stage to premier *The Water Diviner* with a bat in his hand. He placed it against a wall to join the #putoutyourbats bandwagon.

Russell Crowe is an Academy Award winning actor. He is the cousin of cricketers Martin and Jeff Crowe.

91 NEVILLE CARDUS

The 1929 Headingley Test seemed to be hopelessly one-sided at the end of two days.

Neville Cardus left the scene to pursue an affair somewhere close to London.

He didn't watch any play on the third day and discovered the amazing turnaround from the evening papers.

He quickly went to National Liberal Club and composed the match report for the day.

He later described it as one of his best efforts at describing a day's play.

That's what he did so well.

Even Alan Gibson never tried to watch much of the cricket during the day at a ground, but he never bothered to describe the day's play either.

Although he did write beautiful match reports.

In 1985, Andrew Lamb (quite a well-known music historian and occasional cricket writer) revealed in Wisden Cricket Monthly that Cardus was not born on 2 April 1889 but on 3 April 1888.

Three years later, editor David Frith wrote an article to mark Cardus' birth centenary. In that, he recalled the Lamb article and commented that Cardus' autobiography deserved a much better and more appropriate title.

According to him, the autobiography should have been called Unreliable Memoirs—the title of Clive James' autobiography.

No one can deny the fact that Neville Cardus played a huge role in making cricket a popular summer game in England. It was he who helped so many get attracted towards cricket literature. Rather unfortunately, however, not many of them bothered to check what they read. Even with the aid of internet, not many are inclined to verify what had been written by Sir Neville.

Many have tried to set the record straight in the last 30-odd years, but with an appalling success rate.

But, as David Frith hopes (or fears), Christopher O'Brien's new book on Cardus may well shatter his image for all time.

Here's celebrating the man whose cricket writing was all about 'the untruth, the higher truth, and a bit of the truth…'

Neville Cardus is widely regarded as the most famous cricket writer.

92 YABBA

Jack Fingleton divided barrackers into three types (of course he was lucky not to encounter the worst type—who do their bit on social media).

First is the 'blah' type, who always repeats hackneyed comments.

Next is the baiter who rags any person susceptible to barracking—once again unoriginal and monotonous.

The third is the barracking genius. He saves his 'flash of humour' for the right moment, sums up a situation, causes people to 'rock with merriment', and helps many survive the grim and slow passage of play.

Stephen Harold Gascoigne belonged to the third category.

He impressed one and all. Even someone as erudite as Ray Robinson wrote about him: 'Yabba was the only one who stepped forward from the rank of the chorus, so to say, and established himself as an identity. This colloquial wit had a true sense of timing. He had an old soldier's vocabulary, dating back to the South African war, for which he enlisted while on a visit to that country, in his early twenties.'

The cricketers loved him.

C.B. Fry stated that the reason for a trip to Australia was 'to see Australia and hear Yabba'.

Patsy Hendren carried a little red book onto the field of play so that he could note down the comments of Yabba.

When Jack Hobbs played his final match at the SCG, he asked for Yabba—the master batsman shook hands with the master barracker.

Alan McGilvray once estimated that his comments could

be heard once in every fifteen minutes.

Yabba knew how famous he was and he clearly did not regard modesty as a virtue.

In November 1936, he was the subject of a two-minute movie script, in which he said, 'I am the one and only Yabba'.

He once told Arthur Mailey that he was 'the greatest barracker in the world'.

He was present during most matches played in the SCG over a span of 40-odd years.

His great granddaughter Lee Feltham has a nice story to share:

Yabba went blind in later life (sometime after 1937). He could no longer watch cricket and had to be content with hearing the radio commentary.

His grandson was deputed to be his eyes at the cricket.

When Stephen Jr. returned in the evening, Yabba always questioned him about every ball and events during the day's play.

Stephen Jr. usually found himself in trouble if he missed some major event during the day's play!

Yabba, though, always arrived early and watched every ball of the day's play.

Yabba aka Stephen Harold Gascoigne is arguably the greatest barracker in the history of cricket.

93 DAVID FRITH

Then wrote the Queen of England,

Whose hand is blessed by God,

'I must do something handsome

For my dear victorious Stod...'

Well, the Queen couldn't do much for 'victorious Stod', but a certain David Frith did.

They had much in common:
Schooled a long way from their birthplaces, played sports all over the year, married Australian girls, one born 37 years before 1900 and the other born 37 years after (both in March: 11th and 16th respectively), a proximity to Lord's,
...
Stoddart even lived next door to the house occupied by the artist W.P. Frith!
The 32-year-old was so obsessed with the long-forgotten England captain that he had to visit a psychometrist.
He did extensive research to know more about his hero and, in an attempt to find Stoddy's birthplace, he almost died in an accident.
He was sceptical about the book being published.
Publishers, one major and one minor, rejected it after sitting on the typescript and pictures for months.

He had already 'wasted' three years on this project. He had to publish it.
He took a loan of a few hundred pounds from Tony Baer, the Melbourne-based cricket-loving stock investor. Then, he found a printer in Nottingham.

My Dear Victorious Stod came out in 1970. 400 copies. All signed. At £2.50 each.

Then one evening the phone in his house rang.

Jim Coldham from *The Cricket Society* broke the news in a nervous voice. It was some sort of a breach of confidentiality.

The self-published book had won the first ever Cricket Society Jubilee Literary Award.

He told the author not to disclose the secret to anyone else.

Within a few minutes the phone rang again. Another member of the jury. He too said the same thing.

In May 1971, he received the award.

More than 30 books. Founder-editor of arguably the best cricket magazine. Owner of the greatest collection of all things related to the game.

He was the man who first thought and wrote about TV umpires.

It was he who thought and wrote that 'underarm' is quite possible if the opposition needs six off the last ball. Well, he wasn't quite aware of Greg Chappell's reading habits…

Gideon Haigh once told me that there are two places in the world that I must visit.

One is cricket book seller Roger Page's house in Yallambie, a suburb of Melbourne.

The other is David Frith's house in Guildford in Surrey.

The David Frith Archive is a 1100-odd page tome detailing a cricket slave's lifelong collection.

When Sky Sports filmed a short feature on the David Frith Archive a few years ago, the interviewer asked him at the end which his favourite pieces were 'to take to his desert island'.

Frith replied: 'This IS my desert island.'

Slowly but surely, I have moved on from idolising the likes of a Tendulkar or a Lara to idolising the likes of a Frith.

He is 81 at the time of writing and he likes to say 'the clock goes on ticking…'

There will never be another David Frith.

David Frith has been the leading authority on the game over the last fifty odd years. His cricket book and memorabilia collection is unmatched.

94 PETER ROEBUCK

Somerset v Essex
Taunton
September 1975

Essex pressing for the win. Viv Richards and Brian Close both back in the pavilion. Somerset 5 down with a lead of 166.

A 19-year-old bespectacled ex-Cambridge University student, with his competitive nature and technique, trying his best to prevent Essex from wrapping up the innings rather quickly.

Keith Fletcher, the Essex captain, fielding at silly-point to Ray East, summons everyone to 'get Rupert out and we'll be through 'em '.

Everyone else looks slightly perplexed. Stuart Turner asks: 'Who the hell is Rupert?'

'Rupert Pocock', replies the confident skipper.

That nickname stayed with the batsman.

In the county circuit, he was Peter Roebuck to few and Rupert Pocock to many more.

His benefit brochure in 1990 was titled *Rupert's Year*.

'You're like Don Quixote…chasing windmills', once said a certain Scyld Berry.

Roebuck couldn't hold his emotions for a moment but then quickly recovered to say: 'My dad said that to me once when I was young.'

Born English, he enjoyed his days in Greece, became an Australian citizen, bought a house in South Africa, and towards the end of his life, thought of moving to India.

On November 11, 2011, in his final column, he wrote, 'Mind you, a lot can happen in a week. It just did.'

He was right. A lot did happen very quickly—he died the very next day.

David Frith sums it up perfectly: 'Most other people in cricket you can say "What a great bloke. Wish he was still here," or "What a bastard." With Roebuck, it's neither. There has never been anyone like him in my experience, so you can say it was interesting knowing him and I'm sorry it ended that way.'

After his playing days were over, Peter Roebuck became a much-celebrated cricket writer. He later committed suicide.

95 ROWLAND BOWEN

Cricket historian David Frith selected 2,000 pictures from over 50,000 for his *Pageant of Cricket*.

The most difficult to find among them was a picture of Rowland Bowen.

Frith got the picture from the subject's Eurasian wife. It is the only printed picture of Major Rowland Bowen— perhaps the oddest man in cricket's history.

In 1968, he tried to cut his foot off just to show that it could be done. Five years before that, though, he founded the most scholarly magazine on the game. In that, he wrote about his dog, and that they had kissed!

But the content was usually rich. In an era where there were no awards for the best books, the ultimate praise for authors was Bowen's positive comments about their books.

I know someone who had a subscription and when he pointed out in a letter to Bowen that one of the statistical articles made little sense, especially to people from a mathematics background, Bowen became impatient.

The chain of letters ended with Bowen writing: 'I do not know what you mean by shoddy scholarship. I do know your letters are insolent.'

That was Rowland Bowen. Not many knew more about the game than him, but he had his own ways, which often led to quarrels with others.

Murray Hedgcock had plans of writing the Bowen biography, but it was shelved a few years ago.

This man, who got three-line obituaries on an average, deserves a biography.

The good news is that Mr Hedgcock has decided to re-work on this project!

Rowland Bowen was the founder of the scholarly magazine The Cricket Quarterly. *He later wrote a book on the history of cricket.*

96 JOHN ARLOTT

January 1946.

Donald Stevenson, head of the Eastern Service of BBC, asks: 'Isn't there an Indian cricket team coming this summer?'

The man at the other end of the table replies: 'Yes, there is.'

'Oh yes, I remember from your interview that you're keen on cricket. When do they start?'
'First Wednesday in May.'

'Where?'
'Worcester.'

'Where then?'
'Oxford.'

'How do you know?'
'Because I've got the fixture list in my pocket.'

'Have you ever done any cricket broadcasts?'
'Yes.' (the truth was that all he had done before this was a 15-minute talk on Hambledon)

'Would you like to do it?'
'Yes.' (gasps out)

The rest is history.

John Arlott, arguably, is the greatest commentator on the game of cricket.

97 DAVID RAYVERN ALLEN

I remember first reading this name in 2003. There was a mention in an article in *Wisden Asia*. I thought it was the former England off-spinner David Allen.

Then, a few years later (still no internet for me), I got the first taste of a *Wisden* and there was this name again— *Cricketana* by David Rayvern Allen. He wrote that for many years, probably longer than his hero John Arlott's tenure as a book reviewer.

In 1959, he got two offers—one for a pianist for a cruise of the Caribbean and the other for a music arranger for BBC television shows. He chose the latter. He remained there for 35 years.

He wrote many books on cricket—notably, award-winning books on his idol John Arlott and Jim Swanton.

Arlott himself tried to write about his own life. His son Tim tried as well. But no one knew Arlott better than Allen. It resulted in one of the finest cricket biographies.

It was he who suggested the formation of an MCC audio archive. He himself produced all the initial content in the form of interviews with former cricket people.

One of those few who genuinely cared for the game of cricket.

David Rayvern Allen has been a keen student of the game. His books on Arlott and Swanton are admirable. Some say that he knew Arlott better than Arlott himself.

98 GIDEON HAIGH

At the age of 21, Gideon Haigh wrote a book—a business book written by a business journalist.

70,000 words written over a few weekends. When he got a copy in his hand, he read the first couple of paragraphs. There were some silly typographical errors. He never read beyond the first page.

In 1989, he moved to London for a couple of years. The very next year, while watching a boring County Championship match, he thought of trying his hand at serious cricket writing.

He admired David Frith and the kind of work he did at *Wisden Cricket Monthly*. He wrote a piece and posted it to Frith. Within a week, Frith accepted it and published it in the next month's magazine.

Three years later, he wrote a book on Kerry Packer's World Series Cricket. Eleven publishers refused to take it. Then, someone told him about a new publishing house called *Text*. They liked his two-page teaser and agreed to publish it. The book flopped but the author, thankfully, decided to stick to cricket writing.

His *The Summer Game, Mystery Spinner,* and *The Cricket War* are probably among the finest cricket books ever.

In 2010, Richard Whitehead of *The Times* listed *The Fifty Greatest Sports Books*. 49 of those books were easily available in the market. For the 50th, he rang Gideon Haigh.

Haigh borrowed his mother's copy and posted it to Whitehead. A copy of *The Cricket War*.

I have been listing down 'ten favourite cricket books' of cricket writers all over the world and there's been only two who didn't include even one book by Haigh.

One of them is Gideon Haigh.

For the past two decades, Gideon Haigh has been the leading cricket writer in the world.

99 FRANK KEATING

The young man was obsessed with George Lambert, the old Gloucestershire fast bowler.

He modelled his action on him.

He was 17 when this picture was taken. He used to spend hours trying to copy the action perfectly.

He had always wanted to meet Lambert.

His wish did come true but not long before Lambert died.

Frank Keating was a perfectionist.

If he had to know something, he could have done almost anything to find out.

He was a great fan of Jack 'Kid' Berg, the boxer. After waiting for years, Keating finally had a chance to spend a day with him.

The old 'Whitechapel Windmill', 80 and still full of life, whisked Keating at a lick around the East London haunts of his childhood in his little motorcar.

After he won his world title in 1930, he took it to America and defended it successfully 12 times in 12 months.

Jack fought close to 200 contests; many of them were memorable ones.

Yet, that day, he kept asking with exasperation why Keating particularly wanted to know every possible detail about his mundane, non-title victory on points over Glasgow's Jake Kilrain, at the Empress Hall, on 4 October 1937.

That was the night Keating was born. He was very keen to know about every important event that happened on that day.

One of the greatest sports journalists ever.

People who were fortunate to read Frank Keating's pieces miss his writing. They will continue to do so.

100 JOHN LENNON

When Jack Sokell died in 2004, bookseller Christopher Saunders got hold of his collection.

Most of it was letters. Hundreds of them.

Sokell was the face of Wombwell Cricket Lovers' Society in Yorkshire and he corresponded with cricket people all over the world.

The letters were mostly in relation to speaking at the Society's annual programmes. Saunders may even have found a letter written by a 19-year-old man named John Lennon.

Early in 1960, Lennon, along with three others, formed *The Beatles*.

Soon after, they performed at a dance night and caught Sokell's eye.

Sokell wrote to Lennon.

The Beatles agreed to be present in the society's fund-raising dance, provided they were paid £100.

The committee thought that the fee was excessive for a group that no one had heard of.

Sokell, rather reluctantly, agreed and did not go forward with the group.

A month later, *The Beatles* began creating headlines.

Sokell never forgave the committee members.

To his last day, Sokell insisted that he was the one who had really discovered Lennon (*The Beatles*).

And 'imagine' what if the likes of Dickie Bird and Johnny Wardle had agreed to his proposal...

John Lennon of The Beatles was one of the greatest entertainers ever. He was a cricket enthusiast.

ACKNOWLEDGEMENTS

I have been lucky to get the opportunity to interact with some famous cricket journalists and historians.

Kind people, all of them— they tolerated my blabbering. I can't thank them enough.

Here's a short list of people who have helped me with some of the stories I have shared in this book:

Andrew Murtagh

Bill Francis

Christopher Sandford

David Frith

Douglas Miller

Eric Midwinter

Gideon Haigh

Greg Growden

Lynn McConnell

Stephen Chalke

I hope I have not missed anyone's name. My sincere apologies if I did.

A list of books that I read and consulted:

Allan Watkins: A True All-Rounder by Douglas Miller

A Long Half Hour by Stephen Chalke

Beyond Bat and Ball by David Foot

Ball by Ball by Christopher Martin Jenkins

Cricket's Unholy Trinity by David Foot

Caught England Bowled Australia by David Frith

Cricket's Unsung Legend by James Brear

Cricket for South Africa by Jackie McGlew

Cricketing Falstaff by Mark Peel

Cricket: The Game of Life by Scyld Berr

Fragments of Idolatry by David Foot

From Grace to Botham by David Foot

Footsteps from East Coker by David Foot

Great Characters of Crickets Golden Age by Jeremy Mailes

Harold Gimblett: Tormented Genius of Cricket by David Foot

In Sunshine and in Shadow by Stephen Chalke

Jack Fingleton: The Man who Stood up to Bradman by Greg Growden

Lionel Tennyson: Regency Buck by Alan Edwards

Local Heroes by John Shawcroft

Opening Up by Mike Atherton

One More Run by Stephen Chalke

On Top Down Under by Ray Robinson and Gideon Haigh

Pageant of Cricket by David Frith

Playing with Fire by Nasser Hussain and Paul Newman

Rupert's Year (Peter Roebuck Benefit brochure)

Silence of the Heart by David Frith

Shane Bond Looking Back by Shane Bond and Dylan Cleaver

Summer's Crown by Stephen Chalke

Test Outcast by Roy Marshall

The Little Wonder by Robert Winder

The Way It Was by Stephen Chalke

Tom Wills by Greg De Moore

Tom Richardson: A Bowler Pure and Simple by Keith Booth

The Summer Game by Gideon Haigh

The Book of Ashes Anecdotes edited by Gideon Haigh

White on Green by Richard Heller and Peter Oborne

Wisden on Yorkshire edited by Duncan Hamilton

Yabba by Richard Cashman

Zed by Zaheer Abbas and David Foot

10 for 10 by Chris Waters

And now a list of magazines, periodicals, newspapers, and websites that were of immense help:

ACS Journals
ACS website
Between Wickets
CricketArchive
Cricinfo
Cricket Lore
Journal of the Cricket Society
Sydney Morning Herald
The Twelfth Man
The Cricketer
The Times
The Guardian
The Age
Trove
Wisden Cricket Monthly
Wisden Cricketers' Almanack

By chance, if you enjoy reading the book, thank my family (my parents, my wife, and a few other close ones) before you thank me.

They never complained even when I became hell-bent on spending half my monthly income on cricketing stuff.